A Retrospective Study of a Dialogic Elementary Classroom

This book uniquely combines data from a study focused on the use of dialogic instruction in an elementary classroom, with analysis of students' retrospective beliefs about the classroom environment, interactions, and authority.

Through this retrospective methodology, the text offers valuable insight into the long-term impacts of discursive practices on young learners' attitudes to learning and their educational trajectories. Analysis also serves to further understandings of how the classroom environment can function as a living dialogue, in which authority in respect to talk, knowledge sharing, and curricular choices serves as an interactional accomplishment and means of social justice.

This book will be a valuable resource for researchers and academics with an interest in classroom discourse and critical pedagogy. It will be of particular interest to those with a focus on elementary education.

Lynn Astarita Gatto is a retired associate professor and director of Elementary Education at Warner Graduate School of Education and Human Development, University of Rochester, USA.

Routledge Research in Education

This series aims to present the latest research from right across the field of education. It is not confined to any particular area or school of thought and seeks to provide coverage of a broad range of topics, theories and issues from around the world.

Recent Titles in the Series Include:

International Perspectives on Drama and Citizenship Education
Acting Globally
Edited by Nicholas McGuinn, Norio Ikeno, Ian Davies, Edda Sant

Meeting the Challenges of Existential Threats through Educational Innovation
A Proposal for an Expanded Curriculum
Edited by Herner Saeverot

Lived Democracy in Education
Young Citizens' Democratic Lives in Kindergarten, School and Higher Education
Edited by Rune Herheim, Tobias Werler & Kjellrun Hiis Hauge

Multimodal Signs of Learning
Tracking semiosis in the classroom
Shirley Palframan

A Retrospective Study of a Dialogic Elementary Classroom
Understanding Long-Term Impacts of Discursive Pedagogies
Lynn Astarita Gatto

For a complete list of titles in this series, please visit www.routledge.com/Routledge-Research-in-Education/book-series/SE0393

A Retrospective Study of a Dialogic Elementary Classroom
Understanding Long-Term Impacts of Discursive Pedagogies

Lynn Astarita Gatto

NEW YORK AND LONDON

First published 2022
by Routledge
605 Third Avenue, New York, NY 10158

and by Routledge
4 Park Square, Milton Park, Abingdon, Oxon, OX14 4RN

Routledge is an imprint of the Taylor & Francis Group, an informa business

© 2022 Lynn Astarita Gatto

The right of Lynn Astarita Gatto to be identified as author of this work has been asserted in accordance with sections 77 and 78 of the Copyright, Designs and Patents Act 1988.

All rights reserved. No part of this book may be reprinted or reproduced or utilised in any form or by any electronic, mechanical, or other means, now known or hereafter invented, including photocopying and recording, or in any information storage or retrieval system, without permission in writing from the publishers.

Trademark notice: Product or corporate names may be trademarks or registered trademarks, and are used only for identification and explanation without intent to infringe.

Library of Congress Cataloging-in-Publication Data
A catalog record for this book has been requested

ISBN: 978-0-367-64039-2 (hbk)
ISBN: 978-0-367-64040-8 (pbk)
ISBN: 978-1-003-12189-3 (ebk)

DOI: 10.4324/9781003121893

Typeset in Times New Roman
by Apex CoVantage, LLC

For Richie,
who fills my heart with love, joy, and laughter.

Contents

	List of Figures and Tables	viii
	About the Author	ix
	Preface	x
1	Understanding Dialogic Pedagogy: Student Voice, Agency, and Choice	1
2	Interactional Accomplishments in the Dialogic Classroom: Insights From an Elementary Classroom	20
3	A Retrospective Case Study With Former Students	42
4	The Dialogic Classroom in Retrospect: Student Recollections and Long-Term Impacts	58
5	Inclusivity Through Discursive Instruction: Relationships, Social Justice, Belonging	82
6	Living Dialogue and Authority in the Elementary Classroom: Insights to Inform Practice	106
	Index	119

Figures and Tables

Figures

2.1	Framework for Inquiry-Based Pedagogy	24
2.2	Discursive Pedagogy at the Core of an Inquiry-Based Framework	33
2.3	Authority as Forms of Control	36
3.1	Semi-Structured Interview Protocol	47
3.2	Axial Coding Process for the Code Category "Belonging"	51
3.3	Visually Representing the Emergent Theme of Identity	52
3.4	Analytic Memo Exemplar	54
4.1	Graduation Data for RCSD 2012 Cohort	60
5.1	Inclusive Practices for Discursive Pedagogy	98
6.1	Conceptualizing a Living Dialogue	115

Tables

5.1	Defining and Characterizing Relationships	87
5.2	Defining and Characterizing Social Justice	91
5.3	Defining and Characterizing Belonging	94

About the Author

As a veteran elementary teacher in the Rochester City School District, Lynn Astarita Gatto was recognized locally and nationally for her success as an urban educator. Among her many awards, the most notable include the Presidential Award for Excellence in Mathematics and Science Teaching, Toyota Tapestry Award, Disney American Teacher Award, and New York State Teacher of the Year. She is the developer of award winning classroom products. Her innovative teaching practices have been featured in videos and books, including the documentary, *A Life Outside,* a joint production between the local PBS station and the University of Rochester.

Recently, Lynn retired from twelve years in her second career as an associate professor at the Warner School of Education, University of Rochester. She directed the early childhood and childhood master's program for practicing and pre-service teachers. As an extension to her directorship, she also co-founded and held the position of executive director for the first Horizons Summer Enrichment affiliate program on a higher education campus for 135 K-8th grade Rochester City School District students. Lynn has published in both clinical and scholarly journals and she has authored chapters in edited books. Her research interests focus on urban education, classroom discourse, and critical literacy.

Preface

It was two years after the legislation of the No Child Left Behind Act when a group of twenty-one second graders entered my classroom. It was this group of children that would be significantly impacted by this bipartisan law. As students in a failing urban district, they were the target of this legislation. Their success as learners would be measured by high stakes tests. This legislation was the impetus for a whole new market that created and commercialized curricula and products for improving test performance. In response, the traditional discourse of classrooms where the teacher controls who talks, and about what, became even more entrenched. In spite of the large body of educational research that repudiates its effectiveness, teacher-dominated talk became even more embedded as the prevailing discourse style in classrooms, especially in urban classrooms.

This class was to be my last class. I was going to retire at the end of our three-year loop. We were going to be together from second to fourth grade. I was armed with thirty credits of theoretical doctoral coursework, four national teaching awards, numerous local awards, and thirty-two years of anecdotal classroom evidence. I was not about to subject my students to these new forces requiring classrooms to become test prep factories. Nor was I going to end my career managing one!

My non-traditional classroom was one where students did not raise their hands to talk. Instead, they "spoke the way adults do." My urban classroom offered students an approach to learning that was motivated by their needs and interests. The classroom activities and practices were meaningful and engaging. The students read, wrote, and thought mathematically for real purposes. Talk permeated all that occurred in our classroom.

I began my teaching career as a special education teacher, then transferred to the mainstream classroom. After retiring, I administered a nonprofit that offered summer academic/enrichment programming for over a hundred urban elementary students on a university campus. At the same time, at that same university, I taught graduate coursework and directed the early childhood/elementary teacher preparation program. In all of these teaching positions, the students, not the curriculum, drove my decisions for teaching and learning.

Thirteen years after my retirement from my public school teaching career, I still communicated with sixteen of the twenty-one students. I wondered how they remembered the interactions of our three years together. This book describes a retrospective study of that class through an ethnographic lens. The voices of those students twelve years later provide the data which is analyzed to understand the long-term impact of using a dialogic pedagogy. As both the teacher and researcher, I provide a unique perspective. As the teacher, I am an insider. My emic view comes from my own memories of this classroom experience. At the same time, as the researcher, I am an outsider. It is my questions that drive this research and my analysis of the students' interviews that formulates the conclusions. Although researchers are the market audience for this book, there are many teachers who read research. I wanted this book to be accessible and relatable for them too.

1 Understanding Dialogic Pedagogy

Student Voice, Agency, and Choice

My students and I looped for three years, from second through fourth grades. Before we left for summer vacation at the close of our second grade year, we took an overnight trip to Hershey, Pennsylvania. As we entered the town of Hershey, the smell of chocolate permeated our tour bus. We walked through the Hershey Chocolate factory and visited the Hershey Museum. The students posed many questions and their excitement grew to think that we were going to start third grade with the integrated thematic unit, *Yum, Chocolate!*

By the second week of third grade, we were immersed in reading, writing, mathematics, science, and social studies through the topic of chocolate. Fractional chocolate bar mobiles hung from the ceiling. Small group presentation posters depicting the changes for the states of matter in the production of chocolate candy were displayed on the storage cabinet doors. A "Chocolate Shop" was set up on a cart in a corner of the room. Students reviewed money concepts while playing store using fake money to purchase packages of chocolate candies and products. In another corner, a large basket held various chocolate containers for measuring and recording their height, circumference, weight, and volume. On the large bulletin board in the back of the room, books shaped like chocolate ice cream cones exhibited students' creative writing. Brightly colored world maps representing the locations of chocolate growers and producers decorated another bulletin board. Numerous fiction and non-fiction books referencing chocolate were already stored in student book boxes.

As part of this unit, I used books where chocolate was important to the plot for reading instruction. Each morning, the reading instructional block began with a read aloud lesson. Read aloud time occurred on the rug. I sat on a stool and the students sat on the rug or in the surrounding chairs, bean bags, or stools. One morning, as part of the chocolate unit, I began to read the next chapter in *Chocolate Fever* (Smith, 1972). The main character had run away from home and was alone on the street. As I read the last sentence of the chapter, I lowered my voice and read, "He heard a faint sound. It could

DOI: 10.4324/9781003121893-1

have been a dog barking." I paused and looked up from the book, I was about to ask a question. But one of the students yelled, "THAT MEANS THE POLICE!" All at once the entire class burst into conversation and movement. Two boys excitedly stood up, faced each other, and discussed how the police have dogs. The girl sitting nearest them looked up towards them and smiled and then nodded. Four students leaned in towards each other and talked about a possible arrest of the main character. Then, two children interrupted them to disagree that they predicted that the main character was going to be bitten by the dog. Two more students grabbed each other's hands and talked about how one of them had been bitten by a dog. Three students turned and looked toward this group of two and listened. Then one student stood up, came towards me, and spoke to me. He told me that he had been bitten by a dog, and sat back down. I watched and listened.

This outburst of simultaneous overlapping conversation (Gatto, 2001) among my third graders may have seemed chaotic and out of control to any observer. Yet, as I observed the talk and interactions, I noted that children were sharing their background knowledge, making personal connections, and predicting the next event in the story. As soon as I began to speak after this burst of conversation of less than a minute, the class quickly settled into their original positions and focused on my revoicing what I overheard. Then, together we tried to make sense of this surprising end to the chapter. When I closed the book to signal the end of the lesson, all of the students begged for me to continue.

This is just one example of the dialogic events that occurred throughout every day in our classroom community. We were a dialogic classroom community, not only in the context of all subject lessons, but also within small group settings (with and without teacher guidance), among students during independent work times, in one-to-one teacher/student conferences, and during experiences.

The seminal research on dialogic practices in classrooms has identified the forms and functions of discourse patterns (Cazden, 1988; Gutiérrez, 1993; Mehan, 1979; Nystrand, Gamoran, Kachur & Prendergast, 1997). Conceptualizing classroom talk as patterns, or scripts (Gutiérrez), is useful for understanding classroom talk. Dialogic scripts represent "an orientation that members come to expect after repeated interactions in contexts constructed both locally and over time" (Gutiérrez).

Classroom Scripts

Using the participation frameworks of students and teachers, Gutiérrez identified three scripts as the major discourse patterns in classrooms: 1. Recitation Script, 2. Responsive Script, and 3. Responsive/Collaborative

Script. Each script is characterized by speaking rights, roles, and rules, and the social relationships between and among teacher and students. Categorizing classroom talk by participation frameworks is useful in problematizing dialogic approaches through the lens of power dynamics (Freire, 1998; Foucault,1991) and the concept of communities of practice (Lave & Wenger, 1991; Rogoff, 1990). Although these three scripts were identified in the context of literacy lessons, classroom talk conceptualized as scripts is applicable across subjects.

Recitation Script

Gutiérrez (1994) describes the recitation script as a "tightly managed discourse providing limited opportunities for students to produce elaborated talk, especially about topics or subtopics they generated" (p. 341). The pattern of talk in the recitation script is characterized by the teacher controlling the talk and interactions with strict rules for participation. There is a high frequency of teacher-initiated questions with one selected student answering each question. Students have limited opportunities to speak to each other, and are socialized to only produce a correct answer.

This script corresponds to the discourse pattern of initiate, response, and evaluate (IRE) identified by Cazden (1988) and Mehan (1979). The familiar pattern of this classroom script is when the teacher asks a known answer question, the children raise their hands to answer, the teacher calls on one of the students, the selected student gives an answer, and then the teacher evaluates the answer. In IRE only one student is permitted to talk and the student responses are usually one word or a short phrase. The teacher controls what knowledge is privileged through her questions. In this known question/answer script, students are only acquiring factual knowledge or procedural steps rather than becoming meaning makers where they learn to process information, make connections, or create new ideas.

Thus, in classrooms where a recitation script dominates, the teacher decides who will participate and to what extent. The rules are consistent: students must raise their hands for a chance to speak, and the teacher decides who will speak and for how long (Gutiérrez, Larson & Kreuter, 1995). Students are not to interrupt the teacher or another student. Students are expected to remain silent. They participate only when called on by the teacher.

The teacher, in a recitative script, determines who speaks, whose knowledge counts, and what is learned. As the teacher continuously holds the floor, they are positioned as the sole purveyor of knowledge, for which the students are to receive and remember. Facts or procedures are the objects of value in a classroom where a recitation script dominates, not the students. The demands for learning and interaction are low level. Critical thinking, personal experiences, disagreement, or comments are not invited into the recitation script, just the transmission of particular knowledge.

The participation framework for a recitation script results in the marginalization of many nondominant students (Mehan & Cazden, 2015). A tension is created for such students when their cultural and historical ways of speaking and interacting within their homes and communities are ignored or demeaned in the classroom script. Many Black students, for example, are more familiar and comfortable with their oral tradition of "complex music forms, dramatic speech, and imaginative stories" (Smitherman, 1977, p. 101). The call and response discourse from Black churches require the congregation to talk back. These discourse patterns are in direct conflict with the IRE pattern in classrooms. Thus, when Black students try to use their cultural discourse patterns of extended answers, call outs, loudness, laughter, and interruptions they are considered deficient, rude, or as discipline problems.

Second language learners can also be at a disadvantage when an IRE script is used in the classroom. Many second language learners shy away from the public participation of the IRE script because they fear correction of their errors when speaking in their second language of English (Gumbaridze, 2012). Latino/a families often use Spanglish, a form of code-switching from English to Spanish in their homes and community. When students use Spanglish in classrooms, it has been attributed to language incompetence in both English and Spanish (Romaine, 1995).

When a recitation script guides most instructional activities in a classroom, it dictates that the teacher's discourse pattern is the only discourse that matters. The recitation script requires students to echo the teacher's language and curriculum; as a result, that language and knowledge is privileged to be the language and knowledge of power (Delpit, 1995). Since 2001, the No Child Left Behind legislation reinforced the idea of privileging only one right way of communicating and knowing through high stakes testing. These tests are designed to normalize whiteness by expecting students to reproduce white middle class values, a whitewashed history, and white-normed language (Apple, 2000; Au, 2007).

The majority of classrooms around the world spend two thirds of their instructional time using a recitation script (Flanders, 1970; Gage, 1978). Thus, students worldwide are socialized to sit still, speak only when given permission, submit to the rules and regulations imposed by the teacher, and learn only the culturally valued knowledge determined by the teacher's curriculum. Students are indoctrinated into this social system of dominance from the beginning of their education to the end of it. The use of the responsive script makes it clear that students are objects, not subjects of the curriculum and instruction.

Responsive Script

In a responsive script, Gutiérrez notes that students are provided opportunities for contribution and interaction. In this classroom script, the teacher still selects students to speak, but the teacher's questions are not always evaluative in nature; sometimes the questions have multiple answers or are open-ended. Students are also encouraged by the teacher to provide lengthier answers or to expand upon their answer. Sometimes short discussions are held. During a responsive script, the teacher may detour the lesson to a subtopic offered by a student.

Much of the research on classroom talk demonstrates the effectiveness of dialogic talk as a valuable teaching and learning practice, and a responsive script is the first step towards that goal. In many attempts to guide teachers to use a more dialogic approach, professional training programs have been developed. For example, The Thinking Together program (Mercer, Wegerif & Dawes, 2000) is based on Barnes and Todd's (1977) concept of exploratory talk. In exploratory talk students solve problems or come to a common understanding through discussion groups (Mercer, Wegerif & Dawes, 2000).

The Thinking Together program begins with teacher professional development for understanding the goals of exploratory talk. Teachers learn the value of students reasoning together to make joint decisions and how the use of ground rules for speaking together are important aspects of exploratory talk. The teachers learn to use language that will guide and scaffold exploratory talk.

In another example of responsive script professional development, teachers learn to use "talk moves as tools" (Michaels & O'Connor, 2015) for encouraging "equitable and productive" discussion for "supporting robust learning for each student" (p. 334). This Accountable Talk (Michaels, O'Connor & Resnick, 2008) engages students to listen and respond to one another, and in those responses, they make reasoned arguments or connections by applying facts and textual information. From their research, Michaels and O'Connor concluded that five specific talk moves increase Accountable Talk. These five talk moves include 1) revoicing (teacher repeats or paraphrases student statements or questions), 2) repeating (teacher asks student to repeat a statement), 3) reasoning (teacher asks student to apply their own reasoning to another student's explanation), 4) adding on (teacher prompts students for further participation), and 5) waiting (teacher uses wait time for responses).

Finally, in support of advancing a more dialogic approach, many elementary teachers have adopted popular strategies for a responsive script. A widely used strategy is Turn and Talk (also known as Turn to Your Partner or Think, Pair, and Share). The students are asked to turn to a partner and follow the teacher's directions for discussion. The teacher's directions may be to share what they know about a topic, wonder aloud about a new topic, explain their understanding of a concept, use new vocabulary, or defend an opinion. The use of such dialogic tools can become prescriptive and routinized (Lefstein & Snell, 2014).

The demands for learning and interaction in the responsive script are more nuanced than in the recitation script. Using a responsive script is a step towards encouraging a more dialogic approach to teaching and learning. But the teacher is still in full control of the classroom talk and interaction. In a recitation script, the teacher determines when students can talk, how long they can talk, the topic for discussion, and, even, the location of their bodies when they talk. Although there is a nod to intersubjectivity in the responsive script, students are still part of a learning community that is being socialized to learn only the culturally valued knowledge determined by the teacher's tools or strategies for talk and the structured curriculum.

Responsive/Collaborative Script

Unlike an IRE script or responsive script, the framework of a responsive/collaborative script can be described as being more like a conversation (Cazden, 1988). The participation framework in a responsive/collaborative script includes lengthier student answers and uptake, the building of student responses from other students' responses (Gutiérrez, 1994). Gutiérrez also found that students self-select their turns at talking, and multiple opportunities for student participation are afforded. In a responsive/collaborative script, the teacher's participation is as a facilitator and the "discourse and knowledge are more evenly co-constructed" (p. 344).

Nystrand and his colleagues' research expanded Gutiérrez's participation framework for responsive/collaborative script. He described the participation structure as characterized by "dialogic bids." These dialogic bids include 1) talk framed and facilitated by the teacher, 2) turn-taking managed by all participants, 3) sub-topics negotiated by students and teacher, 4) questions initiated and constructed from students' responses, and 5) responses built on previous responses. Nystrand also found that "authentic questions" and "uptake" were essential to creating a responsive/collaborative script. Authentic questions "challenged students to think and reflect on the consequences of their ideas, not just remember their past practices" (p. 73), while uptake connects intertextual uses of students' personal knowledge, classroom knowledge, and texts to the topic. Uptake is when the teacher or students incorporate other speakers' utterances, prior actions, or non-verbal interactions into the classroom talk. It is through uptake that students hold the floor for extended periods (Soter, Wilkinson, Murphy, Rudge, Reninger & Edwards, 2008).

A responsive/collaborative script encourages the negotiation of meaning as students and teacher listen to one another. It also offers students opportunities for constructing instructional topics through interaction and negotiation. Students are also able to ask questions, integrate their cultural knowledge, and pose challenges. It is within this script that students have opportunities to co-construct instructional topics through interaction and negotiation by asking questions, including their cultural knowledge, and challenging ideas. The direction and introduction of topics can be guided by students, as well. The responsive/collaborative script offers a "dialogic stance" where teachers, "listen, lead, follow, respond, and direct" (Boyd & Markarian, 2015, p. 273). It goes beyond using dialogic tools for extending answers and guiding student talk. A responsive/collaborative script mediates learning by leading students to ask their own questions, connect their background knowledge to concepts, stimulate creativity, and promote innovation. It can, at times, be charged with tension and conflict (Gutiérrez, Rymes & Larson, 1995). A responsive/collaborative script embodies a dialogic stance.

Alexander (2020), who has researched elementary classrooms around the world, argues that linking a dialogic stance with best practices must be avoided, and that teachers must base their choices and judgements for dialogic pedagogy using a repertoire of practices. These repertoires are broad concepts of form and function of talk within the context of the classroom activity and culture. Alexander identifies six principles as a repertoire of practices for dialogic pedagogy: collective, supportive, reciprocal, deliberative, cumulative, and purposeful. Alexander argues that these principles guide teachers in the planning and guiding of an effective dialogic classroom. He conceptualizes dialogic teaching and learning as "liberating the voice and thinking of the student" (p. 133).

A responsive/collaborative script allows for a dialogic stance by providing interactional spaces where the students are the subjects, not objects of learning. It is within this script where the teacher and students interrogate concepts, topics, and ideas through multiple voices (Bakhtin & Holquist, 1981). This intersubjectivity signals to students that their voices matter, regardless of their age, gender, race, religion, or economic class. A responsive/collaborative script provides a jointly constructed space for negotiated meanings and problem solving centered on who the students are in the class.

This jointly constructed space allows teacher and students to negotiate the power dynamics within the classroom, where students, not just the teacher, take leadership roles. The co-constructed nature of a dialogic stance empowers students to make connections from the classroom activities to their school and neighborhoods (Tharp & Gallimore, 1988). In a classroom where students matter and are encouraged to communicate, their classroom activities become akin to what happens in the real world. These dynamics also allow for "talking back" to the issues and concerns that the students care about (hooks, 1989). When the responsive/collaborative script becomes an interactional dialogic space, it essentially disrupts the institutional expectations for classroom relationships, standards curriculum, and conversational roles.

The responsive/collaborative script is also a jointly constructed space in which "who gets to learn and what is learned is connected to the social relationships constructed in classrooms" (Gutiérrez, Rymes & Larson, 1995, pp. 466–467). In the context of meaningful activity, a responsive/collaborative script means students are not just "interacting but interthinking" (Mercer & Littleton, 2007). This, then, creates a community of learners where the culture and nature of activities are dialogic. Thus, locating talk in interaction within a community of practice acknowledges that language is a social accomplishment (Ochs, 1988) and provides evidence for understanding how meaning making, social and cultural relationships, identity, and institutional ideologies are mediated.

For this book, the term dialogic is associated with Gutiérrez's concept of responsive/collaborative script. The nature of a dialogic classroom is complex, and since dialogic classrooms are an infrequent occurrence in classrooms around the world, it becomes important to examine dialogic talk in situated classrooms where it does occur. Dialogic talk must be examined from the perspective of how "people within a particular event, act and react to each other in order to understand the social functions and meanings of that participation" (Bloome, Carter, Christian, Otto & Shuart-Faris, 2005, p. 33). It was within my own dialogic classroom that I examined the dialogic interactions.

An Ethnographic Case Study of a Dialogic Elementary Classroom

As a veteran urban elementary teacher, I entered a PhD program which culminated in a dissertation exploring the dialogic interactions within my own classroom. I knew the complex nature of the dialogic interactions in my classroom would provide rich data for a qualitative inquiry. I wanted to understand how student voice operated within our responsive/collaborative script. The data collection occurred over a three-year loop. Student work, over a hundred hours of video recordings of classroom interactions, a personal journal, unit and lesson plans, and transcripts provided a rich data set for my dissertation study. I explored how voice emerged within the responsive/collaborative script in my classroom.

My study examined a literacy event (Heath, 1982) that occurred during the three years we looped. Student voice negotiated a space for naming, analyzing, and subsequently changing a social issue that mattered to them: school lunches. Over 80% of our class qualified for free and reduced lunch, and only one child brought his lunch from home. Everyone else ate the school food. Every single day, upon returning from lunch, someone would make a comment about the food served that day or about an event from the cafeteria. Then, conversation would erupt. They were often angry and hungry. They criticized the recipes used ("They don't know how to make Spanish rice") and the taste of the food (The hamburger is all dry!"). They complained about the lunch cashier who yelled at them to pay their outstanding balances ("I don't have no money! Call my mother!"). They expressed their anger at the mean lunchroom monitors who, abiding by the district rules, forced them to take every menu item offered, prevented them from sharing or trading food, and policed them from taking any food out of the cafeteria ("Look! I snuck this out in my pocket today!").

One day, upon returning to the classroom from lunch, in frustration of the daily complaints, in exasperation, I asked, "So, what are you going to do about it?" This question pushed a larger discussion and it triggered a lengthy project which resulted in the students producing a documentary video to inform the school board and larger community about their plight of school food. They conducted an in-depth study of the school food by authoring and administering a schoolwide student survey, interviewing experts in the field of nutrition and health, and reaching out to neighboring suburban school districts to examine and make comparisons of their lunch programs. Once they synthesized and analyzed all of this data, they scripted, filmed, edited, and produced a documentary video titled, *Lunch is Gross* (www.teachertube.com/videos/lunch-is-gross-11129). After the superintendent saw their documentary, he joined them for lunch the next day and declared, "This lunch IS gross!"

From that point on, our video documentary became the focus for a major drive for change in the lunch program on the part of the school board and the community. As a result of our documentary and other public interactions, a new food service provider was contracted. There were significant changes instituted in the districtwide lunch program. Fourth graders were able to use their critical literacy practices to provoke change in a school lunch program for over 26,000 children.

Throughout the *Lunch is Gross* project, the students and I were forced to confront the relationship between language and power. They received curt and negative responses to their request for lunch menus from a suburban neighboring school district, and pondered the possible reasons. As they compared the monthly menus from the suburbs to their own, they wondered why their menus didn't have pictures, jokes, and fancy names for the menu entrees. When they evaluated the lunch offerings from three nearby suburban districts, they grappled with the huge disparity of salad bars and student choices for a main dish, while they were given no choices, and rarely had salad. A review of district menus revealed that their own district menus offered none of the foods that they ate in their own homes. Their repeated phone calls to the board secretary to request a showing of their short documentary video at a school board meeting was met with delaying responses and rudeness. After the sixth attempt, the students were frustrated and decided to circumvent the board secretary and sent an email with a link of the video directly to each board member. It was at this same time that they also wrote an editorial to the local newspaper, which was printed. The superintendent responded to their email within hours.

Those interactions, along with others, were the impetus for our dialogic learning community to name and reflect upon issues of racism, ageism, privilege, class, oppression, and cultural imperialism. It was also through our responsive/collaborative script that the students and I were able to "engage with local realities, research, and analyze language-power relationships" in order to "mobilize students' knowledge and practices, redesign texts with political, social intent and real-world use, and examine networks of power" (Comber, 2001, p. 276). It was within these responsive/collaborative spaces where the students' voice resulted in choice and agency.

Student Voice

In a critical pedagogy view, the concept of voice is "the speech and perspectives of the speaker," while also "attesting to the right of speaking and being represented" (Britzman, 1989, p. 149). In Freire's (1998) banking model, when teachers deposit knowledge into students' heads, students are objects of knowledge. When students are objects of knowledge, they are voiceless. However, when teachers and students co-construct knowledge, then as subjects of knowledge, students are given voice. With voice, students are allowed to question knowledge, the curriculum, and the inequities in their lives.

It was through classroom talk that we negotiated the meaning of knowledge together, and every student's words mattered. Their voices included the sharing of their everyday home life experiences, articulating their cultural knowledge, and expressing family histories. These funds of knowledge (González, Moll & Amanti, 2005) were especially apparent when they designed the schoolwide surveys and suggested menu items.

The Black and Latina/o students in my class used specific speech genres, which Bakhtin (1986) describes as our everyday repertoire of speech. Half of my students spoke African American Vernacular English (AAVE), which often clashed with the rules of Standard American English (SAE). Around the school, I often heard the teachers and administrators correct and admonish these speech genres telling the students to "speak correctly" or insist a student rephrase their language in SAE. I, however, explicitly presented comparisons demonstrating the parallels between AAVE and SAE. They understood the concept of code switching to the middle class, white speech patterns, and mannerisms for particular times. This ability to code switch, I would remind them, was cultural capital (Bourdieu, 1973) that would help them become successful when participants in the dominant white, middle class culture. However, within the dialogic interactions of our classroom, the voices of their homes were accepted and honored. When writing the *Lunch is Gross* video script, students decided that it would be important to speak in SAE because they knew their audience was comprised of "important people."

Students, particularly non-dominant students, can use their voice to confront and challenge the networks of power that marginalize them, and demand change for equality (Warren & Mapp, 2011). The *Lunch is Gross* project allowed my students to use their voice to transform a deplorable lunch program, endemic in urban school districts, but not suburban or rural ones. Engaging in this project gave them opportunities to question community networks of power in the context of cultural and social practices (Aronowitz & Giroux, 1991).

Having voice in our classroom community also meant my students had the right to express their feelings and question authority. I remember one day I was annoyed at the mess some students had left on a table as we created fruit costumes for the video. I started to clean it up and under my breath I said, "I'm not a maid." One of the students heard me and responded, "We would have cleaned it up. We just didn't have time. YOU made us return to our seats right away." Although many adults may view this as disrespectful, I regarded this as a respectful defense, especially since they were right!

Voice is meaningless if it is ignored. Students will know if their voice is valued as a participant in the learning community when they believe the teacher is listening, acknowledging, and incorporating their voices. They will know their voice matters when they have freedom to use it. In our dialogic classroom, voice became the tool for collaboration, communication, innovation, and creation, which frequently led to choice.

Choice

Offering students choice contributes to feelings of autonomy. Autonomy, according to self-determination theorists Ryan and Deci (1985, 2000) is a basic need, and promotes motivation. However, if choice is to contribute to autonomous feelings on the part of students, then they need to be meaningful choices. Dialogic classrooms do not require every student to speak. There is no selection of a popsicle stick with students' names on them to enforce equality of speaking rights among the entire class. In our community of learners, students always had choice to use their voice.

In fact, there was one student who chose not to speak out loud for the entire first year we were together. He participated in all activities and communicated through body movements like nodding his head or smiling, but he never uttered a word. It was during the taping of the *Lunch is Gross* video where we really heard him speak up for the first time. He was in costume dressed as a cabbage. As he paraded by the camera, we heard him loudly call out "cabbage." The whole class cheered. I remember being stunned.

Students also felt comfortable voicing suggestions to choose alternative approaches for projects. Although I always had the materials organized for use ahead of the lesson, I seemed to be constantly seeking out additional items for students because they wanted to complete the projects differently than I presented. By mid-year of third grade, students had learned the layout of my supply shelves and we negotiated their access to these materials without having to ask permission each time. Thus, having choice often sparked creativity.

But choice was not limited to sparking creativity. During whole group lessons, students frequently asked questions. These questions often led to independent investigations. I remember one student returning from the lunchroom with a small box of raisins. She asked if raisins were really grapes. This prompted her own investigation of four plump grapes in a petri dish. She hypothesized that once the water was evaporated from the grapes, they would become raisins. She kept a daily log for recording size measurements and illustrations of the four grapes in their petri dish over time. Other students became interested in the project and they too would eagerly check the grapes each morning. Sometimes, the other student would remind her to check her petri dish. After two months, she claimed that grapes do indeed turn into raisins. This type of intellectual autonomy occurred easily within our responsive/collaborative script.

Choice also occurred in other ways throughout our classroom talk. Students read independently every day and each student maintained their own selection of reading material for this independent reading time. They could select from a large collection of books, comic books, the daily newspaper, audio books, and informational card collections. Every students' book box was entirely self-selected. Students could be heard recommending or trading books with each other. Often, the books students were reading independently were used to make connections by students during dialogic interactions.

When I gave instructions for an independent assignment or project, students felt free to offer alternative ways of doing the assignment or project. I remember presenting a character analysis project where the students were to include a descriptive paragraph. A student requested that she write a poem instead. Other students thought they might want to do the same. They made the case that they could meet the expectations for the descriptive paragraph. So, the project direction shifted to include poems. Such ideas and requests were always respected and most often realized.

When students used their voice as an opportunity for choice in assignments and projects, they were more motivated and responsible for completing them. Choice afforded students ownership and relevance to the curricular requirements. At the same time, voice within our responsive/collaborative script not only enacted choice, but also empowered student agency.

Agency

Agency is an intentionality towards producing life circumstances, not being the product of them (Bandura, 1996). When students have agency, they critically evaluate their conditions and move towards changing their relationship to those conditions (Emirbayer & Mische, 1998). Dialogic classrooms can allow spaces where students can "struggle in order to make their respective positions heard outside the classroom and in the larger community" (Giroux, 1988, p. 169).

The actions taken to improve school food taught the students much about being change agents. I positioned the students as agents of change when I posed the question, "SO, what are you going to do about it?" The subsequent conversation after posing this question allowed them to voice and weigh their ideas. They learned to weigh their options in terms of impact. They soon understood the importance of using facts and authority in making an argument. They learned to gather data and make their argument compelling. Armed with their argument, they wrote letters to school board members, the principal, the mayor, and the city newspaper. They began to recognize the chain of command within their own school district and their city.

The students also came to understand their own position in this chain of command. As one student put it, "Whose going to listen to us ten-year-olds?" But their letter to the editor published in the city newspaper prompted a local health organization to join forces with us to disseminate and rally the community in the quest for better school food. A large contingent of parents and community members joined the students to protest on the sidewalk of the school district offices. They made signs and then attended a board meeting where a few of the students spoke to the board. It did not go unnoticed, that the white woman from a community organization was able to easily secure time at the board meeting when the students could not. It also became apparent that allies were useful.

I had no plans to produce a video with these students when they agreed among themselves to produce one, but I facilitated their goal. The amount of curriculum embedded in this project covered many aspects from the disciplines of reading, writing, math, health, science, and social studies. But it also went far beyond the state standards for elementary students. I had no intention of facilitating the production of a documentary video, or an organized communitywide protest march. I never dreamed that the students would actually enact such a significant change within our large district.

Our dialogic pedagogy allowed for voice, and from those voices, choice and agency emerged (Gatto, 2012). In this case, student agency is defined by Freire (1998) as the ability for students to "perceive critically the way they exist in the world with which and in which they find themselves . . . and they come to see the world not as a static reality, but as a reality in the process of transformation" (p. 12). This process of transformation for my students meant addressing and taking action against the inequalities they felt they were experiencing themselves.

I recognize voice, choice, and agency as socially and culturally constructed processes for expressing beliefs, shaping ideas, naming realities, and transforming realities. Student agency in our classroom was negotiated and contextual, and it was included in the responsive/collaborative script of our classroom where students had a multitude of opportunities to express their voices, have choices, and become agents of change. The dialogic nature of our classroom also provided a space where the students' cultures, histories, emotions, and personalities became integral to the co-construction of the everyday life of the classroom. What mattered to them mattered to the classroom community.

It was through voice, choice, and agency that authority was represented. Authority is not to be confused with power. Power occurs in classrooms simultaneously with authority as imposed on and exercised from both students and teachers (Foucault, 1980). Thus, power is a process "that structures relationships among people" (Bloome, Carter, Christian, Otto, & Shuart-Faris, 2005) and authority is more closely associated to a "value system which regulates behavior basically because of acceptance of it on the part of those who comply" (Peters, 1966, p. 2). Authority is recognized as an interactional process in classrooms. In the analysis for my dissertation study, authority was conceptualized as three distinct interactional accomplishments: *in* control, *to* control, and *for* control.

Thirteen Years Later

It is now thirteen years since we experienced our looped classroom community. Thirteen years later, the students in that study are now entering their twenties. I am still in touch with many of the students from the class. Most are my Facebook friends. So are their parents. Over the thirteen years, I have received phone calls from certain students and I have met some for coffee or lunch. A few worked for me in a children's summer program I directed on my university campus. One student has even become part of our family. This network of students and parents keep me apprised of their thoughts and activities.

Since those three years in the classroom, I have wondered how the students remember their experiences as a member of our classroom community. I wanted to know if they considered their experiences as having had voice, choice, and agency. I was curious if they remembered the relationship of our classroom talk to authority as an interactional accomplishment. Mostly, I was interested in knowing if our three years together had any impact on their life choices.

This book describes a retrospective case study in order to discover just how our dialogic classroom was remembered and if it mattered beyond the three-year experience. The research clearly demonstrates the advantages of dialogic elementary classrooms. From this rich collection of empirical studies, we know that elementary classrooms using a responsive/collaborative script positively contribute to advancing language and communication (Applebee, Langer, Nystrand & Gamoran, 2003), improving critical thinking skills (Mercer, 2019), and increasing knowledge acquisition (Resnick, Asterhan & Clarke, 2017; van der Veen, de Mey, ven Kruistum & van Oers, 2017).

This book adds to the existing large body of research on dialogic elementary classrooms in three unique ways. First, studies of dialogic pedagogy in classrooms have never used a retrospective case study approach to understand long-term effects of participating in dialogic classrooms. Second, few studies incorporate students' voices into the research of dialogic pedagogy. Third, although many studies on the responsive/collaborative script have used participation frameworks, few have combined it with concepts of authority and group identity.

The chapters in this book elaborate how a responsive/collaborative script, as a dialogic pedagogy, was enacted in my classroom. My last three-year looped classroom in a large, urban district is used as the case in this retrospective study. My ethnographic approach details the students in this class, their memories of their dialogic learning experience, and how, thirteen years later, they viewed the impact of this dialogic classroom experience.

My shift from a recitation script to a responsive/collaborative script is described in Chapter 2. This shift compelled me to articulate a framework for teaching and learning. This framework brings together architecture theory, situated learning theory, and postmodern theory of power and positions dialogic pedagogy central to the framework. Building upon this framework, this chapter details my dissertation study, where the result of the dialogic pedagogy in my classroom became a site for authority negotiation. As a follow-up to my dissertation, this chapter culminates with the questions that drove the retrospective study described in this book.

Retrospective studies are rarely used in the field of educational research. Chapter 3 provides an overview of retrospective research design and the instances of how it has been used in educational research. My own research design is then discussed. The details of my step-by-step process using grounded theory for analysis are also described, exemplified, and justified.

Chapter 4 contextualizes the fifteen students who participated in this study within their city. Rochester has a unique racial and economic history, which impacts each of these students' lives. A short characterization of each student who participated in the study describes them as elementary students and how they presented themselves thirteen years later in their interviews. This chapter also uses the reoccurring themes which emerged from the initial open coding to present a synopsis of the interview data.

Chapter 5 defines and characterizes the three dominant categories that emerged from the data. These dominant categories included relationships, social justice, and belonging. The analysis of six transcript excerpts is used to demonstrate how the definitions and characterizations were derived. The analysis in this case study determined that dialogic pedagogy can be re-imagined to be inclusive and impactful.

In the final chapter, Chapter 6, dialogic pedagogy is re-imagined as a living dialogue using the analysis of this study. It was within the face-to-face interactions of authentic and meaningful classroom activity where a living dialogue emerged. Student voice, choice, and agency developed. The classroom became a place where student authority was valued. A living dialogue was also a space for students to develop caring relationships, be inclusive, and to act for improving their own world. In a living dialogue, the teacher shapes the curriculum and the classroom interactions, but it is the students, through their talk, who enact it. A living dialogue is a co-constructed, interactional accomplishmnet.

References

Alexander, R.J. (2020). *A dialogic teaching companion*. London, UK: Routledge.
Apple, M.W. (2000). *Official knowledge*, 2nd ed. New York, NY: Routledge.
Applebee, A., Langer, J., Nystrand, M. & Gamoran, A. (2003). Discussion-based approaches to developing understanding: Classroom instruction and student performance in middle and high school English. *American Educational Research Journal*, 40 (3), 685–730.

Aronowitz, S. & Giroux, H.A. (1991). *Postmodern education: Politics, culture, and social criticism*. Minneapolis, MN: University of Minnesota Press.

Au, W. (2007). High stakes testing and curricular control: A qualitative metasynthesis. *Educational Researcher*, 36 (5), 258–267.

Bakhtin, M.M. (1986). *Speech genres and other late essays*. (C. Emerson & M. Holquist, Eds. V.W. McGee, Trans.). Austin, TX: University of Texas Press.

Bakhtin, M.M. & Holquist, M. (1981). *The dialogic imagination: Four essays*. Austin, TX: University of Texas Press.

Bandura, A. (1996). Reflections on human agency. In J. Georgas & M. Manthouli (Eds.), *Contemporary psychology in Europe: Theory, research and applications* (pp. 194–210). Seattle, WA: Hogrefe & Huber.

Barnes, D. & Todd, F. (1977). *Communication and learning in small groups*. London, UK: Routledge.

Bloome, D., Carter, S., Christian, B., Otto, S. & Shuart-Faris, N. (2005). *Discourse analysis and the study of classroom language and literacy events: A microethnographic approach*. Mahwah, NJ: Erlbaum.

Bourdieu, P. (1973). Cultural reproduction and social reproduction. In R. Brown (Ed.), *Knowledge, education, and cultural change* (pp. 71–84). London, UK: Tavistock.

Boyd, M. & Markarian, W. (2015). Dialogic teaching and dialogic stance: Moving beyond interactional form. *Research in the Teaching of English*, 49, 272–296.

Britzman, D. (1989). Who has the floor? Curriculum teaching and the English student teacher's struggle for voice. *Curriculum Inquiry*, 19 (2), 143–162.

Cazden, C. (1988). *Classroom discourse: The language of teaching and learning*. Portsmouth, NH: Heinemann.

Comber, B. (2001). Critical literacies and local action: Teacher knowledge and a "new" research agenda. In B. Comber & A. Simpson (Eds.), *Negotiating critical literacies in classrooms* (pp. 271–282). Mahwah, NJ: Lawrence Erlbaum.

Deci, E.L. & Ryan, R.M. (1985). *Intrinsic motivation and self-determination in human behavior*. New York, NY: Plenum.

Delpit, L. (1995). *Other people's children: Cultural conflict in the classroom*. New York, NY: The New Press.

Emirbayer, M. & Mische, A. (1998). What is agency? *American Journal of Sociology*, 103 (4), 962–1023.

Flanders, N.A. (1970). *Analyzing teacher behavior*. New York, NY: Addison-Wesley.

Foucault, M. (1980). *Power/knowledge: Selected interviews and other writings 1972–1977*, ed. C. Gordon. New York, NY: Pantheon.

Foucault, M. (1991). Space, knowledge and power. In P. Rabinow (Ed.), *The foucault reader*. Harmondsworth, Middlesex: Penguin.

Freire, P. (1998). *Pedagogy of the oppressed*. (M. B. Ramos, Trans.). New York, NY: Continuum.

Gage, N.L. (1978). *Scientific basis of the art of teaching*. New York, NY: Teachers College Press.

Gatto, L.A. (2001, April 10–14). *Simultaneous Overlapping Conversation (SOC): A theoretical framework* [Conference presentation]. AERA 2001 Convention, Seattle, WA, United States.

Gatto, L.A. (2012). *Negotiating authority through whole class talk.* Unpublished doctoral dissertation. Rochester, NY: University of Rochester.

Giroux, H. (1988). *Teachers as Intellectuals: toward a critical pedagogy of learning.* Westport, CT: Bergin & Garvey.

González, N., Moll, L.C. & Amanti, C. (Eds.). (2005). *Funds of knowledge: Theorizing practices in household communities, and classrooms.* Mahwah, NJ: Lawrence Erlbaum.

Gumbaridze, J. (2012). Error correction in EFL speaking classrooms. *Procedia– Social and Behavioral Sciences*, 70, 1660–1663.

Gutiérrez, K. (1993). How talk, context, and script shape contexts for learning to write: A cross case comparison of journal sharing. *Linguistics and Education*, 5 (3 & 4), 335–365.

Gutiérrez, K. (1994). Ethnic studies curricula. In *Encyclopedia of English studies and language arts* (Vol. 1, pp. 467–468). Urbana, IL: National Council of Teachers of English.

Gutiérrez, K., Larson, J. & Kreuter, B. (1995). Cultural tensions in the scripted classroom: The value of the subjugated perspective. *Urban Education*, 29 (4), 410–442.

Gutiérrez, K., Rymes, B. & Larson, J. (1995). Script, counterscript and underlife in the classroom: James Brown versus Brown v. The Board of Education. *Harvard Educational Review*, 65 (3), 445–471.

hooks, b. (1989). *Talking back: thinking feminist, thinking black.* Boston, MA: South End Press.

Heath, S.B. (1982). What no bedtime story means: Narrative skills at home and school. *Language in Society*, 11 (1), 49–76.

Lave, J. & Wenger, E. (1991). *Situated learning. Legitimate peripheral participation.* New York, NY: Cambridge University Press.

Lefstein, A. & Snell, J. (2014). *Better than practice: Developing teaching and learning through dialogue.* London, UK: Routledge.

Mehan, H. (1979). *Learning lessons: Social organization in the classroom.* Cambridge, MA: Harvard University Press.

Mehan, H. & Cazden, C. (2015). The study of classroom discourse: Early history and current developments. In L. Resnick, C. Asterhan & S. Clarke (Eds.), *Socializing intelligence through academic talk and dialogue* (pp. 13–34). Washington, DC: AERA.

Mercer, N. (2019). *Language and the joint creation of knowledge: The selected works of Neil Mercer.* Abingdon, UK: Routledge.

Mercer, N. & Littleton, K. (2007). *Dialogue and development of children's thinking: A sociocultural approach.* London, UK: Routledge.

Mercer, N., Wegerif, R. and Dawes, L. (2000). *Thinking together: A programme of activities for developing speaking, listening and thinking skills for children aged 8–11.* Birmingham, UK: Imaginative Minds Ltd.

Michaels, S., O'Connor, C. & Resnick. L.B. (2008). Deliberative discourse idealized and realized: Accountable talk in the classroom and in civic life. *Studies in Philosophy and Education*, 27 (4), 283–297.

Michaels, S., & O'Connor, C. (2015). Conceptualizing talk moves as tools: Professional development approaches for academically productive discussions. In L. B. Resnick, C. Asterhan, & S. N. Clarke (Eds.), *Socializing Intelligence through Talk and Dialogue* (pp. 333–347). Washington DC: AERA.

Nystrand, M., Gamoran, A., Kachur, R. & Prendergast, C. (1997). *Opening dialogue: Understanding the dynamics of language and learning in the English classroom.* New York, NY: Teachers College Press.

Ochs, E. (1988). *Culture and language development: Language acquisition and language socialization in a Samoan village.* Cambridge, UK: Cambridge University Press.

Peters, R.S. (1966). The authority of the teacher. *Comparative Education*, 3 (1), 1–12.

Resnick, L.B., Asterhan, C.S.C. & Clarke, S. (2017). Student discourse for learning. In G.E. Hall, D.M. Gollnick & L.F. Quinn (Eds.), *Handbook of teaching and learning*. Hoboken, NJ: John Wiley & Sons.

Rogoff, B. (1990). *Apprenticeship in thinking: Cognitive development in social context.* New York, NY: Oxford University Press.

Romaine, S. (1995). *Bilingualism*. Oxford, UK: Blackwell.

Ryan, R.M. & Deci, E.L. (1985). *Intrinsic motivation and self-determination in human behavior.* New York, NY: Plenum.

Ryan, R.M. & Deci, E.L. (2000). Self-determination theory and the facilitation of intrinsic motivation, social development, and well-being. *American Psychologist*, 55, 68–78.

Smith, R.K. (1972). *Chocolate fever*. New York, NY: Puffin Books.

Smitherman, G. (1977). *Talkin and testifyin: The language of Black America.* Detroit, MI: Wayne State University Press.

Soter, A.O., Wilkinson, I.A.G., Murphy, P.K., Rudge, L., Reninger, K. & Edwards, M. (2008). What the discourse tells us: Talk and indicators of high-level comprehension. *International Journal Educational Research*, 47, 372–391.

Tharp, R.G. & Gallimore, R. (1988). *Rousing minds to life: Teaching, learning, and schooling in social context.* Cambridge, UK: Cambridge University Press.

van der Veen, C., de Mey, L., van Kruistum, C. & van Oers, B. (2017). The effect of productive classroom talk and metacommunication on young children's oral communicative competence and subject matter knowledge: An intervention study in early childhood education. *Learning and Instruction*, 48, 14–22.

Warren, M.R. & Mapp, K.L. (2011). *A match on dry grass: Community organizing as a catalyst for school reform*. Oxford, UK: Oxford University Press.

2 Interactional Accomplishments in the Dialogic Classroom

Insights From an Elementary Classroom

The class roster for my last group of students consisted of twenty-one students, of which five were white, six were Latinx, and eleven were Black. All but two students received free and/or reduced lunch. Four were English Speakers of Other Language (ESOL) students supported by pull-out services for three hours a week. For two, their native language was Bosnian and for the other two it was Spanish. Seven students received daily one-hour pull-out support for speech and learning disabilities as mandated by their IEPS (Individualized Educational Plans). After the first year, at my suggestion, the special education support teacher pushed her instruction into our classroom instead of pulling these students out. Two children had medical diagnosis for behavior disorders but received no support services. Four of the students had already repeated either first grade or kindergarten.

During the two weeks before school started, I visited every students' house to meet them and their families. I explained the concept of looping to them and that this classroom would not be a traditional one. Instead, the students and I would approach learning from utilizing real-world experiences and talk. I explained that we would use trade books instead of the reading series, writing for real purposes would replace writing workbooks, and instead of learning science facts, science concepts would be experienced through hands-on lessons. Math would be taught conceptually using manipulatives. I also explained how I viewed the importance of field experiences as integral to learning, which would include overnight trips. I assured each family there would be no cost for any these experiences. Instead, the students would earn the funds as a class. Finally, I expressed my own philosophy for learning as inquiry which necessitated much classroom talk. I forewarned parents that they should not expect a quiet environment when they visited.

The first day of school was spent deciding how to brand ourselves. The class agreed to name themselves, *The Explorers*. Our class motto became "spending the next three years together as we explore our world through

DOI: 10.4324/9781003121893-2

reading, writing, math, science, and social studies." An image of Henry Hudson's sailing ship became our logo. He was also the Explorer for whom our school was named. We created business cards for each student and class stationary headlined with our new logo and motto. This branding involved much discussion and decision making.

Therefore, I immediately introduced the idea of how they could talk in a group without raising their hands. Even though they had only been in school for two years, the students were already socialized to raising their hands and speaking only when called on by the teacher. I explained that we would speak "the way adults do," gaining the floor when there was an opening. I shared my belief that learning happened through talk, not just my words but theirs, too. I emphasized the importance of listening and speaking to each other, not just to the teacher. I introduced possible actions that effective speakers and listeners use. These actions included: wait for an opening to begin speaking; look at the speaker; think about what the speaker is saying; hear the speaker out; and get to the point when speaking. I also introduced the kinds of phrases to use when responding to one another, such as: excuse me; I'd like to add; I disagree; I don't understand what you mean by; I'm confused by; and I'd like to add that.

In the first months of school, I reinforced the expectations and roles of "speaking like adults" through role-playing and modeling. Most effective, however, was the viewing of whole class or small group discussions that I had video-taped. Watching video of themselves was a powerful tool for reflecting on the practices needed for an effective dialogic classroom. Our repertoire of dialogic practices began to take shape. Although there were always interruptions, side conversations, and simultaneous overlapping conversations, taking turns at talking among the twenty-two of us was always productive and mostly respectful.

My classroom didn't always operate this way. I began my career as a traditional teacher who used IRE discourse almost exclusively. But my belief system for classroom engagement shifted dramatically during my twelfth year of teaching. I transferred to a school within my district that had recently been selected to participate in the *New York State Systemic Initiative for Math, Science and Technology*. Ten elementary schools from across the state were to become research and development sites for inquiry-based instruction, specifically through math, science, and technology. The funding provided professional development, mentor support, and resources. During the three years of the grant, teachers were expected to shift their instructional methods so that their students would learn firsthand knowledge of mathematical and scientific concepts by exploring, asking questions, and conducting investigations, with the goal of communicating and articulating with one another about their new knowledge. Inquiry was the theoretical framework for this initiative (New York State Education Department, 1997).

I participated in statewide professional development for the entire summer before the transfer to my new school. We spent time exploring science concepts as inquiry learners ourselves. I was provided with numerous books and articles to read. A personal science content coach, who was a professor at a nearby university, was assigned to me as my mentor. I entered my new classroom with apprehension, excitement, and a resolve to let go of old beliefs, especially the commonly long-held belief that the teacher needs to control everything in the classroom.

It was my participation during this first summer of the statewide initiative where I began to rethink my approach to classroom talk. If children were going to ask questions and work together to find solutions or answers, and then articulate their findings, there was going to be a lot of talk going on. I wanted my students to be able to talk with each other, and as a whole group. I wanted my students to ask meaningful and productive questions about the topics we were learning. I wanted my students to begin to construct their own understanding and knowledge of the world by experiencing the world through hands-on and real-life interactions. Learning was no longer going to be something I did *to* my students. Instead, it was going to be something I did *with* my students. That would require not talking *to* my students but *with* my students.

As a result of my participation in the initiative, my entire way of thinking about teaching and learning shifted. My classroom no longer operated where the students were the consumers of my fun and engaging learning activities. Instead, I came to believe that teaching and learning happened as my students and I produced knowledge, and a dialogic classroom would lead to that production of knowledge.

I was elevated to a Lead Teacher position and my classroom became a demonstration site for district teachers to visit. I published articles for the state education department, and provided districtwide professional development. I won many local and national teaching awards. A few years after the initiative ended, I enrolled in a doctoral program. I missed the intellectual conversation the initiative had provided. I wanted to learn more. It was in the PhD program where I discovered the field of dialogic pedagogy and the concept of a theoretical framework for teaching and learning.

One Teacher's Theory of a Dialogic Classroom

My own instructional shift to inquiry theory grew out of science and math instructional professional development, which was framed on constructivist learning theory, and I viewed its possibilities as a framework for all of the subjects I taught within the elementary curriculum. Two literacy teachers, Short and Burke (1996), wrote about their own experience of adopting an inquiry framework for their literacy classrooms and how it required a shift of their entire belief system about teaching and learning. Their theoretical shift included the ways in which they viewed the curriculum, their students, and how teaching and learning should occur. I, too, went through this same theoretical shift.

At first, I thought the physical space of my classroom was the necessary change. For a classroom based in inquiry teaching and learning, there would have to be accessibility to materials and equipment. Work spaces needed to be available for children to conduct explorations and investigations in small groups. There needed to be spaces for collections of artifacts, student book boxes, communal supplies, manipulatives, and on-going projects. But the furniture also needed to be arranged in ways that would be conducive for whole group as well as small group conversations. I envisioned one-to-one conversations would take place too.

I realized that much more was needed than just a physical change. I began to think more deeply about my goals for teaching and learning. Up until this point, I had given little thought to basing my own classroom practices in philosophical theory or educational research. I was a bandwagon jumper, jumping from one teaching fad or trend to another. I delved into theory and research. As a result, I developed a theoretically based framework for teaching and learning (Figure 2.1).

My framework integrated theories from the fields of architecture, social learning, and postmodernism. Architecture theory considers a built environment to include aesthetics and adaptability to human activity. Social learning theory conceives learning as a social experience that is contextually situated, while postmodernism positions power and authority relative to knowledge. Central to my framework was discursive pedagogy. I knew all of the theories I attached my beliefs to would correlate to classroom talk.

Theory of Architecture

Architects design spaces using atmosphere as their framework. This requires that they ask the following questions: In what ways will the space function? In what ways will human interactions occur? What multisensory aspects will evoke emotions, associations and memories?

Zumthor (1999) is one of the most revered architects of the 21st century. He considers these questions in his approach to architecture of buildings. He describes his philosophy of architecture as the creation of physical space, which suggests an immediate emotional feeling as a room is entered. He determines which materials will be compatible with one another to

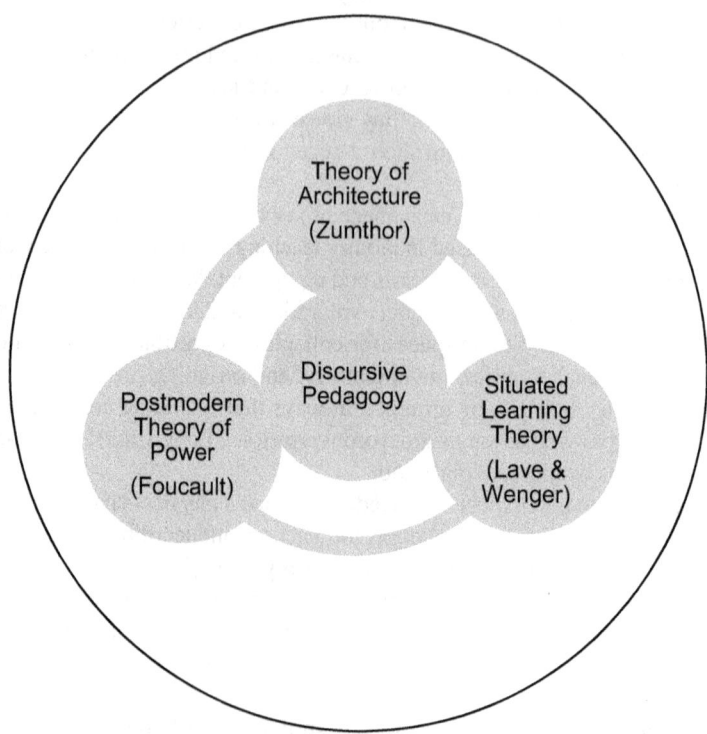

Figure 2.1 Framework for Inquiry-Based Pedagogy

create the desired feeling of the space. The sound of the room, the temperature, and objects surrounding the space are also important considerations for Zumthor. He aspires to have the inside spaces of his buildings provide the feeling of being enclosed in a special place, where it feels as though the occupants are being held together by the architectural environment.

He also believes there should be a tension between interior and exterior. He believes that the outside of the building should not present all that it is, and that entering the inside spaces offers a deeper statement. When he contemplates his architectural designs, Zumthor also thinks about the levels of intimacy, or proximity and distance. This requires the architect to consider who will be entering the space, and engage them through a personal feeling within that space, while also providing the feeling of being part of the whole group who enters.

Zumthor's concepts for creating atmosphere – spaces with a distinctive character for inspiring an emotional connection – were the same concepts I considered when creating the classroom environment for teaching and learning through inquiry. I wanted anyone who entered the classroom, and especially my students, to immediately think, "Something different is going on here." I wanted my classroom to have the atmosphere of a special place, an interesting place, a place where any student would want to spend lots of time. I wanted my classroom to invite my students to come in and inquire.

Designing the physical space of my classroom for atmosphere involved much planning and creative thinking. I began by arranging classroom furniture to offer whole group, small group, and individual interactions. The twenty-one student desks were positioned to form a large rectangle, and among this configuration of student desks sat my own child's-sized desk. Inside this rectangle, a few short stools were scattered about. This way student dyads could work across a desk and the open floor space also offered room for small groups to spread out. It also allowed me to work one-to-one with students as I could quickly move from desk to desk from inside the rectangle. A few tables were also stationed around the room to offer other places so I could guide small group instruction or for small groups of students to work together.

The classrooms' cinder block walls, fiberglass-tiled ceiling, and long fluorescent lights offered only an impersonal institutional feeling when one entered the classroom. I wanted to transform it into a welcoming and exciting place for children. I chose a nature theme for the classroom decor, and used compatible materials to create this theme. Through my arrangement of bookcases and picket fencing, I created a variety of spaces and nooks to erase the cinder block walls. One such space was the classroom library created by bookshelves placed perpendicular to the walls. These shelves housed over a thousand organized books and other reading material. The cages of the tarantula, the tortoise, and the gerbils were placed along the top of the low bookcases. This was the space that also hosted many of our whole-class lessons on the rug. But not all students were comfortable sitting on the rug, so I created alternative choices for seating. One of these choices was on top of a storage trunk which held a treasure trove of costumes and masks. It was made into a comfortable seat with a vine-printed cushion. A rocking chair painted with vines and flowers and four small picnic benches also offered seating choices.

On the other side of the library was the computer corner. I installed a large L-shaped counter into the wall where the four computers were placed. Eight stools underneath the counter invited students to work together at the computers. Anyone who entered the room was greeted by a large park bench decorated with flowered pillows. Beside the bench was a large turtle pond with picket fencing used to create a partition. On the other side of this fence, a large wicker barrel chair offered a cozy spot near the shelves that housed labeled storage containers of science equipment and tools. The snake's cage sat eye-level on those shelves, and a bookmaking supply shelf was butted against the back side of that shelf. Across the room, a tall shelf stood against a wall near the student desks, which held a wide assortment of labeled storage containers full of math manipulatives. A gooseneck lamp clamped to the top shelf of this bookcase shone down on a stool placed alongside it. This served as the "Spotlight on the Author" stool where students took turns sharing their original stories with the class.

There were built-in bookshelves that lined the lower half of one whole wall. These shelves held shoe boxes and plastic bags of art supplies for various projects and were hidden from view with curtains made from flowered patterned fabric. The counter above these shelves provided storage for the students' projects of the moment, and this long shelf was bookended by two large fish tanks.

Just as Zumthor denoted the importance of the sound, temperature, and objects surrounding the space, so did I. The nooks and crannies of the room offered sound proofing and quiet spaces. Gentle bubbling from the fish tanks and water gliding over the filtering system in the turtle pond provided soothing background noise all day long. Living plants hung from atop the tall bookcases. The room was illuminated by torchiere floor lamps, table lamps, and natural light from two large windows in order to avoid the harsh glare of the fluorescent lights. A large tree stump served as both a table and a stool. Student work hung from the branches of a dead tree. It all worked to create a comfortable and cozy feeling within the classroom.

Zumthor's theory argued that tension should exist between the interior and exterior of a building; tension also was manifested within my school building and my classroom. The entrance to my school was through a full wall of glass panels two stories high. Upon entering, the open feeling of the building immediately stopped. An overhang from the second floor cut off the natural light and the entrance became dark and cold. The walls of this hallway were unpainted cement blocks and poured cement panels. The immediate feeling was cold and impersonal. Although colorful bulletin boards displayed friendly and welcoming messages throughout the hallways, it did little to evoke any warmth in the gray and dark hallways. But entering my classroom immediately evoked a sense of warmth and color; it was an aesthetic experience walking into my classroom.

Community of Learners Theory

The physical environment, or architecture of my room, was also designed to create a sense of community. A community of practice has a shared domain of interest, and the members mutually participate in a goal-directed joint enterprise. This mutual participation requires a negotiation of the meanings of their actions in order to develop or create a shared repertoire (Wenger, 1998). In the case of my classroom, I viewed our domain of interest as exploring and inquiring to learn about the world around us. It was within this domain of interest that we could learn from one another and value the collective expertise among the community members as we participated in joint activities. Wenger views relationships as integral to the community. He posits that over time and through sustained interactions, the members of the community share a joint repertoire of resources and develop shared practices that constitute their ways of doing things.

The idea that creating a community of practice takes time was profound for me. Just as the class began to develop strong relationships with one another, develop a joint repertoire of practices, and begin to act like a community of practice, the school year would be over. For seven years, I begged my principal to let me loop with my class, preferably for three years. I presented the many educational and social/emotional advantages of looping with the same students, but she argued that would force the other teachers to switch grade levels. Finally, when a new principal was assigned to my building, he enthusiastically granted me permission to loop, and I was able to loop for the last nine years of my career.

Building upon Wegner's situated learning theory, Rogoff (1990) conceptualized the idea of a community of learners for classrooms. Rogoff's concept is grounded in the socio-cultural theory where learning is viewed as a change in participation. This understanding of learning differs from the transmission model where children are asked to prove that they have acquired specific facts and knowledge, or from the discovery model where children learn what interests them on their own. In a classroom that is a community of learners, learning becomes a change in participation when students and teacher collaborate to learn a curriculum in relation to their world. In each of these models children learn the curriculum, but in a socio-cultural model the curriculum becomes meaningful to the students and is regarded in relation to the shared repertoire of practices within the classroom. This shared repertoire can consist of classroom practices that include rituals and routines, the way in which they use tools, stories of the classroom community, and the everyday talk.

To make learning meaningful and expand our repertoire of practices, I developed four ten-week thematic units of study for each school year. Each theme was aligned to my district's grade level curriculum, but I did not use the district textbook or guidelines for instruction. Instead, I developed units where the theme directly connected to math topics, reading strategies, communication processes, and science and social studies concepts. Field experiences were integral to making the topic come alive. Each unit was driven by a culminating activity where students would demonstrate their newly acquired knowledge and changes in participation.

One such unit was based on New York's history standard for learning about the Indigenous people of New York, the Iroquois. My unit, titled "The Haudenosaunee," (the French named them Iroquois; however, the tribe's actual name is Haudenosaunee) connected to many of the skills, strategies, and concepts that were required in the fourth-grade curriculum. As our community of learners began an in-depth exploration of the daily life and history of the Haudenosaunee, we read accounts of early Haudenosaunee life, visited museums to view archaeological artifacts, took a trip to the historic site of the largest Seneca village of the 17th century, and heard from present-day clan members about the life of their ancestors and present-day life. A large chart displayed the ongoing list of the questions they asked while participating in these first-hand experiences. It was from this list that small groups of students chose topics for their own research. Each group decided how they would distribute their new knowledge throughout the learning community. They presented puppet shows, skits, a song, and PowerPoints.

Math and science concepts were learned through the planning and planting of a Haudenosaunee's Three Sisters Garden, comprised of the three most important crops of corn, beans, and squash. A daily read aloud of the chapter book *The Indian in the Cupboard* (Banks, 1980), in which the main character is a boy, about the same age as my students, brings his plastic toy Indian to life using his magic cupboard. Throughout the story, the boy uses his cupboard to bring other toys to life, most notably a cowboy who has many conflicts with the Indian character. The idea of three-inch tall people inspired the creation of miniature dollhouses where students used math and science to design and create two small rooms with furniture to scale, while also applying concepts of circuitry to electrify them.

As a culminating activity to the unit, the children created a museum to which the other students were invited. Every one of the museum exhibits were innovated, designed, and created by the students. The students served as the docents for the museum and each was dressed in the Haudenosaunee traditional clothing designed and sewn by themselves. The museum featured a walk-in long house, a buzzer board game to match the parts of a flower, and demonstrations of Haudenosaunee dances. The students performed their plays, puppet shows, and songs. Visitors were invited to read the published class book of legends authored by the students using authentic Haudenosaunee legends passed down through the generations as mentor texts.

As our community of learners became immersed in actively learning about and thinking about the Haudenosaunee, the students and I shared in the roles of expert. There were many instances of children assisting one another and working together in small groups. Some students became experts in sewing the clothing and helped others. I may have determined the theme and the idea of the culminating activity, but my students drove many of the lesson ideas and activities through their questions, personal stories, and comments.

The objectives for this unit went beyond the required literacy curriculum. The storyline of *The Indian in the Cupboard* (Banks, 1980) was the perfect text to think about critical topics. The characters in this story are stereotyped using racializing language. This led to many conversations whenever such stereotypes occurred in the story. My Black and Latino/a students were astute to these occurrences and had many opinions and personal connections about those issues. One student made the connection to slavery when we read of the young boy owning the Indian. When a woman Indian is brought to life to make the male Indian happy, the girls in the class immediately objected. As the students learned about the earlier everyday life of the Haudenosaunee, the students pointed out the inaccuracy of the author's facts.

Each thematic unit presented similar opportunities for immersion into a topic. Certainly, they learned to refine and develop new practices related to the district curriculum. But they also, investigated their own questions, critically interrogated and analyzed texts, and produced texts of their own. They also developed an awareness of how networks of power impacted their histories, their present lives, and others around the world. I planned three thematic units for each year. Each one lasted about twelve weeks. Each theme was developed for connecting multi-subject objectives to the topic. All of the thematic units were based on the state standards topics for science and social studies curricula.

The dialogic repertoire of our classroom community allowed students to relate their personal experiences, ask questions, and share their ideas, which helped them to connect the curriculum and their own identities. Their questions and ideas were good ones. Their questions not only helped me to understand what they didn't understand, but also to understand who each student was as a person. I often listened more than I talked, and my listening allowed for a space where the students offered productive ideas for investigations and curricular shifts that were meaningful to them.

This dialogic approach was the most significant shared repertoire of practices in my classroom. Throughout each unit of study, the students and I negotiated how and what we would learn through talk. The thematic units provided a mutual participation for a goal-directed joint enterprise which furthered our shared repertoire of practices. Rogoff differentiates a community of learners from other learning models using the nature of student participation. She describes student participation in a community of learners as developing relationships with one another as they work to accomplish a common endeavor. With each unit presented, my students built upon the last unit to shift their participation as learners and members of the community. This shift in approach to teaching and learning also meant a significant shift in the network of power relations within the classroom.

Postmodern Theory of Power

When power is considered in relation to classrooms, it is often associated with the teacher in the position of authority. In this belief, power is exercising one's will over others (Weber, 1947) and thus, as a repressive mechanism, the teacher exercises power over each student. But according to Foucault (1998), "power is everywhere" (p. 63) and is circulated and represented by discourse. Discourse serves to "prescribe particular rules and categories which define the criteria for legitimating knowledge and truth" (Adams, 2017, para. 2). These discourses or "regimes of truth" are the valued techniques and procedures within the power network (Foucault, 1991). A regime of truth, then, is "the strategic field within which truth is produced and becomes a tactical element in the functioning of a certain number of power relations" (Lorenzini, 2015, p. 3).

In worldwide educational systems, the regime of truth has become a discourse of standardization and compliance. Most countries utilize curricular standards and high stakes testing, which serve to rank and sort students (Salaky, 2018). Students around the world are controlled by the expectation of sitting still and listening to the teacher, speaking only when called upon, providing short answers to teachers' questions, and maintaining silence as instructional tasks are completed. Students conform throughout each school day as bells signal the beginning and ending of school. The school schedule dictates when students have special classes (gym, art, and music), recess, and meals and even sometimes bathroom breaks.

In the United States, along with high stakes testing, report cards, disciplinary logs, testing data wall charts, and national/state standards are all aspects of instructional control. Teachers and the administration often threaten students with grade retention if they do not score well on tests or demonstrate the maturity required for the next grade. The teachers are provided with and expected to use textbooks, workbooks, test prep materials, and supplemental programs for remediation. All materials and curriculum are focused on preparing students for standardized testing.

These networks of power for discipline, control, and standardization in my school had become normalized and part of the everyday discourse. Most teachers and students align themselves with this "regime of truth" for this competitive and dominating discourse on schooling. But my framework for inquiry-based teaching conflicted with the dominant discourse for schooling. The concept of looping for three years avoided the idea of failing a grade level. I committed to my students and their parents that no one would be excluded from our community of learners during those three years for any reason. The integrated thematic units I created challenged and rejected the district-mandated materials for instruction and the preparation for standardized testing. Although each thematic unit included subject standards, I did not use the instructional approaches the district expected. Nor did I use the materials provided by the district. Instead, I used trade books, artifacts, manipulatives, and field experiences which were financed by writing grants, award money, or by my own money. I employed culturally relevant and individualized instructional approaches.

A few weeks before I began a new thematic unit, I submitted a narrative document detailing the upcoming unit to my principal. Every unit began with an introduction to the theme and a graphic organizer demonstrating how all subjects' goals and objectives would be addressed through the theme. Then, a detailed explanation provided a timeline and a description of the materials, books, activities, guided reading groups, field experiences, and culminating project for the unit.

But our classroom community was not an island and the institutional networks of power did impact me and the students. When my school instituted a schoolwide behavior program that rewarded tickets for compliant behavior, I told my students I would not be participating in this program. I explained that they already knew how to behave and I was not going to hand out tickets for doing what they already knew. I explained that I would honor anyone who wanted to save their tickets from the other teachers. Only a handful of students saved their tickets, but after their first trip to the office to exchange their tickets for a prize, they returned and shared how insignificant the prizes were and how "stupid" the program was. As part of this same behavior program, each teacher was assigned two specific times during the day to take the entire class to the bathroom. My colleagues would call me out or report me to the principal for non-compliance of this rule. I refused to regulate when children were to go to the bathroom.

At the beginning of each new school year, stacks of classroom workbooks and textbooks were readied for each teacher on an assigned lunchroom table. I taught in the school for fourteen years and each year the vice principal would come to my room a few days before school started and ask me when I was coming to get my books. Each year I reminded her I didn't use them and she should not have bothered to order them for me. I also reminded her that I never put in a book order at the end of the year. After a few years, she had the school custodian deliver the books to my classroom and he laughed when I told him to, "Just put them in the bookroom." He said he knew I would tell him that. Finally, the vice principal gave up trying to force me to take the textbooks.

The nature of the classroom dialogic interactions in my classroom, however, caused the most tension within our institutional network of power. The classroom architecture immediately signaled a shift in power relations for teaching and learning to anyone entering the classroom. The classroom's floor plan resisted the institutional architecture of traditional classroom where the teacher surveils the students from her position at the front of the room. Instead, the front of the room shifted throughout the day and was defined by the activity. Rarely did I stand at the front of the classroom and frequently, when a guest, administrator, or parent entered the classroom, they would look about and ask a nearby student, "Where's your teacher?" The architecture of my classroom was not designed for student discipline or control, but to engage them as a community of learners.

The conversational floor demonstrated negotiated participation structures and rules. My classroom was a space where children often led discussions, answered one another's questions, and felt free to connect their own cultural practices or knowledge to the conversation. Our conversational floor had rules that differed from every other classroom in the school. Children did not raise their hand to speak. When one child dominated the discussion, either other students or I would remind them to let others have a turn at speaking. Sometimes, the students' talk would overlap one another or side bar conversations and interruptions would occur. But these out-of-turn interactions were almost always connected to the topic of the conversation and purposeful.

The adults in my school viewed the dialogic practices in my classroom as "uncontrolled," "undisciplined," and "unconventional." The other adults in the school that interacted with my students constantly complained to me about their poor listening skills and rude behavior, and often a student or two would be sent to the office with discipline referrals for "calling out answers" or "talking to other students." My administrators and colleagues viewed the nature of dialogic interactions in classrooms from a "regime of truth" that is used to constrain and regulate students. This "regime of truth" also served to "perpetuate the existing status hierarchy and reinforce social inequity" (DeSena & Ansalone, 2009, p. 60). In a school such as mine, where Black students were the dominant population, the punishment of my students' talking infractions normalized and privileged the dominant discourse patterns favored by the middle, class white culture (Delpit, 1988, 1995; Smitherman, 1977).

The "regime of truth" for schooling has had a strong impact on the discursive practices of schooling, particularly associated with behavioral and communicative roles of students and teachers. However, the participation frameworks used for our inquiry-based communicative practices resisted the educational "regime of truth." Within our classroom's network of power, we created our own "regime of truth" through our discursive practices.

Discursive Pedagogy

Discursive pedagogy was at the core of my inquiry-based framework for teaching and learning (Figure 2.2). Mutually constituted spaces for discursive opportunities would be created by interacting within a designed physical environment, functioning as a community, and understanding power as productive. Students would know they were in a classroom community where they would talk to learn. Their talk would encompass their sharing of personal experiences and background knowledge, making connections among themselves, arguing, agreeing and disagreeing with each other, offering ideas to the community, questioning texts, sharing grievances, and expressing personal feelings. Students' voices were central to this framework. From their voices, agency and choice would emerge.

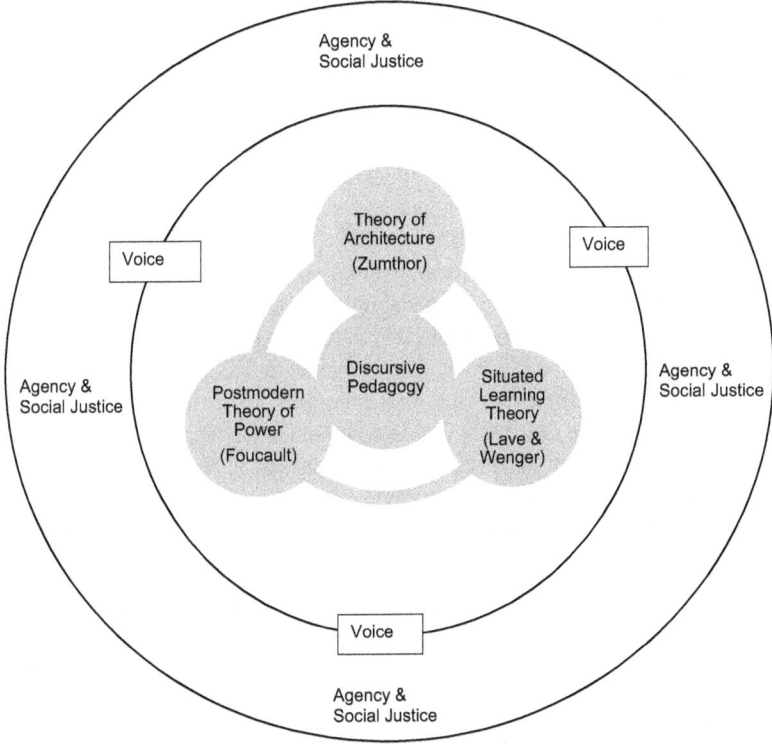

Figure 2.2 Discursive Pedagogy at the Core of an Inquiry-Based Framework

In an early issue of Dialogic Pedagogy (2014), Matusov and Wegerif, two leading researchers in the field of dialogic pedagogy, debated their positions on dialogic education. Both believe in education THROUGH dialogue, and agree that "education through dialogue is not in itself dialogic education" (p. E1). However, Matusov argued that his view of dialogic education is a genuine dialogue, not a contrived dialogue for meeting specific curriculum goals. For him, the focus of dialogic education is on personal responsibility and agency. Thus, dialogic education, in his opinion, is education FOR dialogue and where dialogic learning "is always emergent and unpredictable" (p. E1). Essentially, Matusov argues that classroom dialogue should lead the curriculum. Instead of curriculum being used for cultural indoctrination, dialogic pedagogy creates an education where culture is created.

In contrast, Wegerif argued that Matusov "seems to want to 'corrupt' conventional monologic practices and push subversively the conventional education into the dialogic realm," in order to "arrive at some important curricular endpoints preset by society" (p. E4). In his response to this summary of his position, Wegerif wrote, "In my view dialogic education is not student centered, nor is it teacher centered, but it is dialogue centered. The dialogue of humanity that education serves is bigger than the interests of particular students and particular teachers. It has its own logic and if we allow ourselves to be open to its voice, we find that it calls us all forward in an open ended way on an exciting adventure" (p. E19). He articulated his stance that dialogic pedagogy is education AS dialogue and believes that teachers "can design environments and experiences" for the "process of shared inquiry" (p. E17).

Discursive pedagogy from an inquiry-based framework is closely aligned to Wegerif's view on dialogic pedagogy. I was obligated by contract to teach the required curriculum, but this didn't mean I should ignore student interests, questions, and their funds of knowledge.

Wegerif views the teacher-dominated monologic talk in most classrooms, as "an authoritative voice that closes down dialogue" (p. E 18). Instead, he asserts Bahktin's notion of "persuasive voice" gives teachers the authority to "engage students where they are and draws them into dialogue in a way that leads to further dialogue" (p. E 18). Authority, then, comes from the shared participation of dialogic pedagogy.

Forms of Authority

Authority is not to be confused with power. Power occurs in classrooms simultaneously with authority as imposed on and exercised from both students and teachers (Foucault, 1980). Thus, power is a process "that structures relationships among people" (Bloome, Carter, Christian, Otto &

Shuart-Faris, 2005). Authority, on the other hand, is more closely associated to a "value system which regulates behavior basically because of acceptance of it on the part of those who comply" (Peters, 1966, p. 2). Peters makes a distinction between two types of authority (1) *an* authority and (2) *in* authority. *An* authority is associated with knowledge expertise, while *in* authority indicates maintaining the conditions for order. Peter's understanding of *in* authority recognizes the interactional processes of authority as shared participation.

Building upon Peters conception of authority, Oyler (1996) argued that the two dimensions of authority are content and process. This aligns to Peter's conceptions of authority. Using discourse analysis, Oyler identified classroom talk in her second grade classroom where authority was shared between herself and her students. She concluded that when students are allowed to initiate and take control of questioning, they become positioned as both *an* authority and *in* authority. My dissertation built upon, further developed, and extended Peter's and Oyler's conceptualization of authority.

Conceptualizing Authority in One Dialogic Classroom

My dissertation began with a broad question for understanding the nature of whole-class talk within my classroom community. Grounded in a three-year data corpus, authority emerged as a major theme. I wanted to understand the ways in which the dialogic spaces of our classroom mediated authority. Conversational analysis provided the tools for a micro-analysis to theorize the dynamics of how authority shaped and was shaped within our whole-class talk. I selected one particular nine-minute video clip of whole classroom talk centering on the *Lunch is Gross* project (Gatto, 2013). I transcribed every turn at talk based on Jefferson's (1984) transcription conventions.

The analysis sought to understand how the teacher and students used communicative resources to negotiate these three forms of authority during whole class talk. This detailed form of analysis allowed me to conceptualize authority in three forms: *in* control, *to* control, and *for* control (Figure 2.3). It is through the participation structures and negotiated rules of the conversational floor that makes each one distinct.

In Control

To understand authority in the form of *in* control, an analysis of the conversational floor was conducted by counting the number of occurrences to compare teacher and student turns of talk, topic initiations, simultaneous turns of talk, and latching turns in the transcript. Initially this analysis revealed that I was *in* control of managing the topic selection and managing

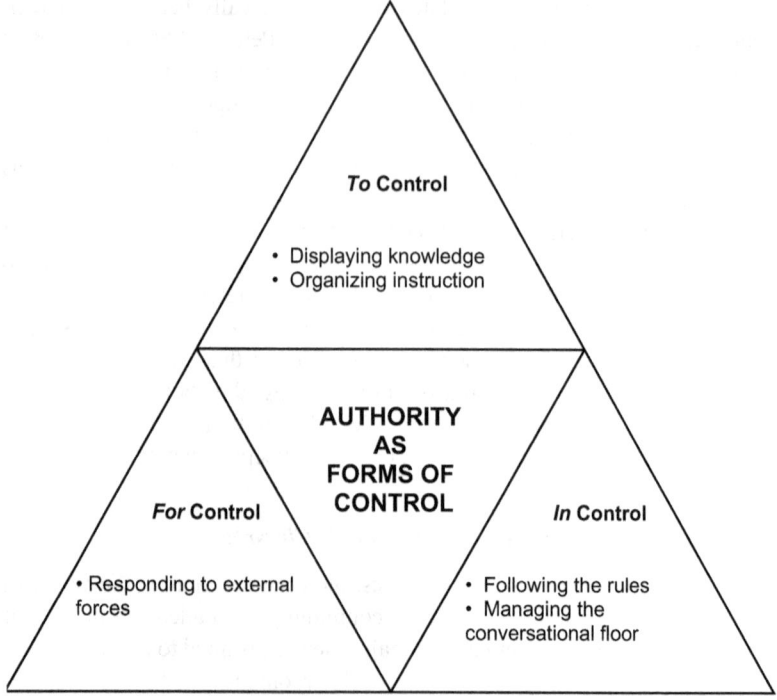

Figure 2.3 Authority as Forms of Control

the conversation, although there were examples of students admonishing someone to be a better listener ("You're not listening to me") and the uptake of new topics introduced by students.

A deeper analysis of the transcript, however, revealed that the students and I negotiated the authority to be *in* control on the conversational floor. Students held the floor for long periods of time, latching onto each other's statements. In one segment, a student asks me a question and other students respond. There are also occurrences where I tried to return to a topic, but the students continued their discussion instead, and after a few turns of talk, a return to the topic was picked up by a student.

There were many rituals and routines that I initiated in our classroom community. Some of which centered on the ways that classroom talk was conducted. Bossert (1978) suggests that the teacher's authority is maintained through the practice of routines and rituals. However, the Explorers often contributed ideas for new rituals or routines, or offered ideas to improve them. I also found that the students monitored the rituals and routines for themselves and each other. From my analysis, authority in the form of *in* control describes the jointly negotiated processes and structures that managed classroom actions, classroom rules, and the conversational floor.

To *Control*

In the ethnographic case study, I positioned my dialogic interactions *to* control what knowledge was significant while, at the same time, giving students opportunities to find conversational spaces for their cultural and personal knowledge *to* control what knowledge was significant to them, particularly when it came to meal preparation and menu items.

I exercised my authority *to* control the organization of dialogic instruction, while the students also negotiated and found spaces *to* control their own sense of organization for instruction. In one example, a student initiated a new topic and I interrupted this student in an attempt *to* control the instructional focus but added an "OK?" as I looked at the student when I interrupted. This was a purposeful negotiation between myself and the student. In another example, I directed the students to take out a marker and highlight certain aspects of the lunch menu. All of the students became quiet and followed the direction. This signaled that they had confirmed the teacher's authority *to* control the organization of the instruction. However, the menu also included breakfast choices and students vocalized their desire to look at those too. I commented, "We can only do lunch!" accompanied by a smile. Many of the students laughed. No one brought up breakfast again. I had successfully negotiated a limit to our project.

IRE was at times a script within this classroom's interactions, but I was not the only one to use it. Students used it *to* control the transmission of knowledge they wanted to acquire from me. For example, the students were looking at the school menu; it listed chicken w/ French fries. A student initiated a questions to the teacher, "What does the w/ mean?" I responded that the "w" meant with. The student then evaluated my answer with, "Oh OK." The dialogic interactions in this classroom positioned the authority of the teacher and students *to* control what counts as knowledge, who is knowledgeable, and how instruction is organized. The transcript analysis offered insight into how the forms of authority *to* control were either jointly negotiated or mutually agreed upon by all of us.

For *Control*

Analysis of the transcript revealed that students used the conversational floor as a space to use their authority *for* control. The turns of talk were explored, my turns frequently longer in words than that of the students' turns, except when the students' talk took on the authority *for* control. A portion of the transcript revealed an example of this when a student loudly interrupts the conversation with an unrelated topic. She complained about a lunchroom policy ("They make us take the food, even if we don't want it."). Then, two more students used extended turns to support her statement. Their voices, too, were elevated, which signaled that this topic was an emotional one for them. I relinquished the current topic and asked, "What do you mean?" Then I looked at one student who began to speak, followed by others. Because the volume of the students' voices became normal, it may have indicated to the students that I valued their issue. The turns at talk in this exchange averaged twenty-four words, while my own ranged from one to eleven words.

The students used this dialogic exchange *for* control of an issue that mattered to them. Perhaps we would be able to act upon it. The issue of forced food distribution became a huge issue for many of the students. The day after this conversation, they took it upon themselves to take action on their own. When I arrived to pick up the class from the lunchroom, almost half the class had been sent to the office. To avoid the rule of taking every part of the lunch, they snuck out of the kitchen and went directly to the lunchroom. When the students were directed to go back into the kitchen to get their lunches, they refused and were then sent to the office. The documentary included this issue. Authority *for* control can be characterized as the teacher and students reacting and acting to the network of power when it is deemed as unfair or unjust.

Authority as a Negotiated Accomplishment

The analysis and findings suggested that authority is visible in three forms of control 1) *to* control, 2) *in* control and, 3) *for* control throughout our dialogic interactions. The Explorers' dialogic interactions were often mediated by all three forms of authority. Being *in* control, positioning *for* control, or attempting *to* control fluidly moved throughout the whole class talk. For the Explorers, authority became a negotiated accomplishment during dialogic instruction that fluidly moved from one form of control to another.

The majority of the dialogic interactions described and analyzed for this study was unlike the recitation script which serves to maintain the teacher as *an* authority and *in* authority (Peters, 1966). Instead, the whole group talk in this classroom was an interactional accomplishment in which authority was jointly negotiated and socially constructed. The whole class talk demonstrated that the forms of authority created symmetrical and asymmetrical relationships between myself and the students, but also within the power networks of the school and district.

As the Explorers jointly negotiated forms of authority in their dialogic interactions, critical literacy practices emerged. Critical literacy positions students and teachers as active participants in exploring together the relationship between language and power within real life contexts to understand how the world is socially, historically, culturally, and politically constructed and how it operates (Anderson & Irvine, 1993; Luke & Freebody, 1996). The goal of critical literacy, according to Freire (1970), is through dialogue. Students develop conscientization, that is, identifying social injustices and taking action to change them. Critical literacy requires students and teachers to "insert themselves and their texts into public spheres" (Lensmire, 2000, p. 64). As students gain an understanding of how the networks of power can be recognized through language in the form of text, speech, and multimodalities, they become empowered to act.

A Retrospective Study as a Follow-Up

My dissertation study took place when high stakes testing and reductionist curriculum reached a pinnacle, especially for urban elementary students. The research demonstrated that providing urban elementary students with a space for dialogic pedagogy resulted in negotiating authority between and among the students and the teacher with critical literacy practices as the outcome. These negotiated forms of authority resulted in critical literacy practices. Critical literacy theory is shaped from critical pedagogy where the focus is on "generating knowledge that presents concrete possibilities for empowering people" (Giroux, 1988, p. 103).

The goal of critical literacy is to go beyond just the mechanics of reading and writing and develop a "critical consciousness" (Freire, 1998), and position students as active participants in exploring, together, the relationship between language and power within real-life contexts. Together, teacher and students seek to understand how classrooms, schools, neighborhoods, and cities are socially, historically, culturally, and politically constructed and how they operate (Luke & Freebody, 1996). As students gain an understanding of how power is recognized through language in the form of text, speech, and multimodalities, they can "question power relationships, discourses, and identities in a world not yet finished, just, or humane" (Shor, 1999, p. 2), and then "to take action against the oppressive elements of reality" (Freire, Friere & Friere, 2004, p. 35).

The making of the documentary became an authentic literacy learning project. Students used their voice to critically explore an issue that they cared about and wanted to change. They challenged the power relationships between themselves and the food services management and the adults in charge of the school district. In and of itself, that made this a critical literacy project. Janks (2010) refers to this as using critical literacy to deal with "the daily politics with which children identify" (p. 190). As an outcome of a dialogic pedagogy, critical literacy became a way for the students to use negotiated forms of authority to question the discourses and decisions of the school and district.

But did the implementation of discursive pedagogy from an inquiry-based instructional framework have any long-term impact on the Explorers? Did the dialogic classroom, where authority was a negotiated interactional accomplishment and instructional practice become critical, have any influence on the ways in which they engage in the world now, thirteen years later? If so, in what ways? How do the Explorers remember the dialogic experiences? In what ways do they remember authority being negotiated? As a follow-up to my dissertation study, I conducted a retrospective study to seek the answers to these questions.

References

Adams, R. (2017). *Michel Foucault: Discourse*. Retrieved from https://criticallegalthinking.com/2017/11/17/michel-foucault-discourse/.

Anderson, G. & Irvine, P. (1993). Informing critical literacy with ethnography. In C. Lankshear & P.L. McLaren (Eds.), *Critical literacy: Politics, praxis, and the postmodern*. New York, NY: State University Press.

Banks, L.R. (1980). *The indian in the cupboard*. New York, NY: Doubleday.

Bloome, D., Carter, S., Christian, B., Otto, S. & Shuart-Faris, N. (2005). *Discourse analysis and the study of classroom language and literacy events: A microethnographic approach*. Mahwah, NJ: Erlbaum.

Bossert, S.T. (1978). Classroom structure and teacher authority. *Education and Urban Society*, 11 (1), 49–59.

Delpit, L. (1988). The silenced dialogue: Power and pedagogy in educating other people's children. *Harvard Educational Review*, 58, 280–298.

Delpit, L. (1995). *Other people's children: Cultural conflict in the classroom*. New York, NY: The New Press.

DeSena, J. & Ansalone, G. (2009). Gentrification, schooling and social inequality. *Educational Research Quarterly*, 33, 60–75.

Foucault, M. (1980). *Power/knowledge: Selected interviews and other writings, 1972–1977*. New York, NY: Pantheon Books.

Foucault, M. (1991). *Discipline and punish: The birth of a prison*. London, UK: Penguin.

Foucault, M. (1998). *The history of sexuality: The will to knowledge*. London, UK: Penguin.

Freire, P. (1970). *Pedagogy of the oppressed*. Harmondsworth: Penguin.

Freire, P. (1998). *Pedagogy of the oppressed*. (M.B. Ramos, Trans.). New York, NY: Continuum.

Freire, P., Freire, A.M.A. & Freire, P. (2004). *Pedagogy of hope: Reliving Pedagogy of the oppressed*. London, UK: Continuum.

Gatto, L. (2013). "Lunch is gross": Gaining access to powerful literacies. *Language Arts*, 90 (4), 241–252.

Giroux, H.A. (1988). *Teachers as intellectuals: Toward a critical pedagogy of learning*. Boston, MA: Bergin & Garvey Publishers.

Janks, H. (2010). *Literacy and power*. New York, NY: Routledge.

Jefferson, G. (1984). On the organization of laughter in talk about troubles. In J.M. Atkinson & J.C. Heritage (Eds.), *Structures of social action: Studies in conversation analysis*. Cambridge, UK: Cambridge University Press.

Lensmire, T.J. (2000). *Powerful writing, responsible teaching*. New York, NY: Teachers College Press.

Lorenzini, D. (2015). What is a "regime of truth?" *Le Foucaldien*, 1 (1). Retrieved from https://foucaldien.net/articles/abstract/10.16995/lefou.2/.

Luke, A. & Freebody, P. (1996). The social practices of reading. In S. Muspratt, A. Luke & P. Freebody (Eds.), *Constructing critical literacies* (pp. 227–242). Creskill, NJ: Hampton Press.

Matusov, E. & Wegerif, R. (2014). Dialogue on "dialogic education": Has Rupert gone over to the "dark side"? *Dialogic Pedagogy*, 2. Retrieved from https://doi.org/10.5195/dpj.2014.78.

New York State Education Department. (1997). *Mathematics, science and technology resource guide*. Retrieved from www.p12.nysed.gov/guides/mst/.

Oyler, C . (1996). *Making room for students: Sharing teacher authority in Room104*. New York, NY: Teachers College Press.

Peters, R.S. (1966). The authority of the teacher. *Comparative Education*, 3 (1), 1–12.

Rogoff, B. (1990). *Apprenticeship in thinking: Cognitive development in social context*. New York, NY: Oxford University Press.

Salaky, K. (2018). *What standardized tests look like in 10 places around the world*. Retrieved from www.insider.com/standardized-tests-around-the-world-2018-9.

Shor, I. (1999). What is Critical Literacy? *Journal of Pedagogy, Pluralism, and Practice*, 1 (4), Article 2.

Short, K.G. & Burke, C. (1996). Examining our beliefs and practices through inquiry. *Language Arts*, 73, 97–104.

Smitherman, G. (1977). *Talkin and testifyin: The language of Black America*. Detroit, MI: Wayne State University Press.

Weber, M. (1947). *The theory of social and economic organization*. (A.M. Henderson & T. Parsons, Trans.). Mankato, MN: The Free Press.

Wenger, E. (1998). *Communities of practice: Learning, meaning and identity*. Cambridge, UK: Cambridge Press.

Zumthor, P. (1999). *Thinking architecture*. Boston, MA: Basel.

3 A Retrospective Case Study With Former Students

Retrospective case studies are ones in which the researcher looks back to understand a phenomenon. Retrospective case study designs are characterized by three features: 1) data collection occurs after the event being studied, 2) first person accounts and historic data are used, and 3) the final outcome is already known (Street & Ward, 2012). In retrospective studies, timelines of events are often reconstructed after the events have occurred.

Retrospective case studies are commonly conducted in the medical, psychology, and management fields. Retrospective study design provides a systematic process for reviewing existing data that is easily available, which gives access to longitudinal information. The medical and psychology fields use historical patient records, doctors' notes, and interviews to understand the influence of interventions after they have occurred. The management field use databases and interviews to reflect upon and identify past planning processes or organizational and strategic changes.

Retrospective case studies have been criticized for their limitations when used in the medical and systems management fields. Retrospective case studies can be time consuming because interviewing participants and scrutinizing records can be a lengthy process. It may also be difficult to obtain records long after the events have occurred. In one large systems management study, it was discovered that the participants had vague memories or attempted to cast their past behaviors in a positive light (Golden, 1992). But these limitations are mitigated by the fact that retrospective case study designs are usually small-scale studies and also provide voice to the participants involved.

Retrospective Case Study in Educational Research

The use of retrospective case studies in education is limited. There are a few examples of educational studies using a retrospective case-controlled study design. This means that a comparison of cases with and without a

DOI: 10.4324/9781003121893-3

condition of educational interest are identified and then compared retrospectively between the two cases. For example, a retrospective case-control study design was used to understand the effects of offering school readiness services to pregnant women and young children since 1993. A comparison of those receiving services and those who did not was conducted fifteen years after the start of the program (Pozzi & Lotyczewski, 2008). Pairs of students were matched using gender, district, school, and grade and then the specific data was compared retrospectively. They used a wide range of school records and assessment scores as their data set to compare health indicators and school outcomes.

In other retrospective studies using a case-control design, the analysis of student attendance records compared early elementary student cohorts with chronic and regular absences. Such comparisons were found to be indicators of which students would drop out of high school (Hess & Copeland, 2001). Snipes and Casserly (2002) also used a retrospective case-controlled study to compare urban districts across the country to determine which were making improvements in academic and racial disparity. They began this study by retrospectively analyzing state assessment results to identify the districts making the most gains, then three districts were selected as cases to determine what resulted in the success of those districts.

The majority of retrospective case studies in education are frequently used to understand the impact of a specific professional development experience on teaching practices in the classroom. Cohorts of teachers are often asked to retrospectively consider how their experience impacted the implementation of a major instructional change initiative within their classrooms. These retrospective studies have explored significant changes in practices for teaching writing (Gamble, 2007), reading (Anderson, 2009), and science (Ufnar, Bolger & Shepherd, 2017).

Conner's (2012) retrospective case study explores the long-term implications of research conducted in schools where the educators disputed the outcome of the research. She interviewed eight original participants from both the public high school and the research institution, from a study over twenty-five years ago. From the semi-structured interviews, she recognized that the teachers who participated in the original study had strong negative memories and opinions about the resulting publications and research institution. The memories left little impact on the researchers, which had faded.

While retrospective case study design has provided opportunities for teachers and researchers to retell or reflect back on their experiences as educators, very few exist using students' memories. One study explored how engineers were motivated to choose their profession based on their elementary school experiences (Strutz, 2012). In another, the cultural experiences of students who faced the effects of desegregation policy were examined

(Gersti-Pepin, 2002). While there have been retrospective case studies designed to understand student learning from the perspective of the learners, these have all occurred with college or high school students (Abbot & Cameron, 2020; Brock & Wiest, 2012; Tamir & Amir, 1981; Tidwell & Edwards, 2020).

I conducted an exhaustive search for retrospective studies that used the memories of elementary school students to understand the impact of practices for teaching and learning. I have found none.

Understanding Students' Memories

The retrospective case study approach for this research detailed in this book used my former students' memories to determine how they remembered and perceived their experience in a dialogic classroom. This study is unlike any others. It uses the memories of students to understand the dynamics and impact of participating in an elementary dialogic classroom.

Research Design

Qualitative research methodology focuses on the ways in which people make sense of, and develop meaning from, their experiences in the world in which they live. It is the intent of the qualitative researcher to describe, examine and interpret those experiences (Bogdan & Biklen, 1992), and understand the meaning of those lived experiences.

After thirteen years, I wanted to understand the memories of those students who were highlighted in my dissertation work. Thus, I continue to identify this group of students as a case. Case study according to Stake (2000) "is not a methodological choice but a choice of what is to be studied" (p. 435). The outcomes of this case study are intended to (1) study the dialogic classroom experience as one case, (2) identify and understand the memories of the contextual conditions of the case, and (3) extend the outcomes of the case beyond just the case (Yin, 2003).

When I first conceived of this study, I was still in my position at the university as an associate professor. I completed the application required by my institution's review board to review research. This was to assure my research subjects' rights and welfare would be protected. After the board reviewed my research plan and protocols, it was approved.

Participants

There were twenty-one students, and after our three years together, I retired from my thirty-four-year career as a teacher. Since my retirement, I have maintained contact with most of the Explorers. I have been invited to their homes for dinner with their families, met some for breakfast, and spoken to many on the phone. I am friends on Facebook with eighteen of the Explorers and also twelve of their mothers or siblings.

I began this study by reaching out to the Explorers I was friends with on Facebook by contacting them using Facebook Messenger. The message I sent out read:

> It has been thirteen years since you were an Explorer. You may remember that I videotaped many of our classroom activities and conversations in order to understand the talk in our classroom when I was working on my doctorate degree. As many of you know, I retired from teaching elementary school and am now teaching classes to current and future teachers at the college level. As a professor, I am also conducting research. My current study wants to understand how you remember your experience as an Explorer. I hope to interview any Explorer that can contribute an hour of their time using ZOOM or Google Meet. I would like to record each interview. Once I have interviewed everyone who wants to participate, I will analyze your interviews and come to some conclusions about teaching and learning. I hope to write a book about this study. Your name or pictures of you will not be used in any publications about this study. Please respond as soon as possible using Messenger.

Seven students responded within the first hour of the message being sent. The other positive responses arrived over the next few weeks. One of the students did not have a Facebook account, but his mother works in a restaurant I frequent. She connected us, and he agreed to participate.

One student declined to participate. She responded that she was, "Not in a mental health space where I feel as if I will be able to help you." She recently transitioned from male to female and posted on her Facebook page that she was seeing a doctor for depression. Two of the students who I was friends with on Facebook did not respond. I checked their Facebook pages and it was clear their accounts had been inactive for over three years. They did not have any other social media accounts using their real names, so I was unable to locate them.

In all, I had fifteen of the twenty-one students who agreed to participate in the study. It was not easy scheduling twenty-one year-olds for one-to-one interviews. Many times, I would send the ZOOM invite at the agreed-upon time and there would be no response. They would later apologize and offer a variety of reasons for missing the appointment ("I forgot" "I got called into work" "The baby was acting up" and "My phone was dead.") After four months, I was finally able to conclude all of the interviews.

Using interviews in a retrospective study affords rich and detailed qualitative data for understanding participants' experiences, how they describe those experiences, and the meaning they make of those experiences (Rubin & Rubin, 2012). A protocol for the semi-structured interview was used consisting of open-ended questions (Figure 3.4). Semi-structured interviews are used to gather focused, qualitative textual data. This method offers a balance between the flexibility of an open-ended interview and the focus of a structured ethnographic survey. A semi-structured interview also "allows for considerable reciprocity between the participant and the researcher" (Galletta, 2013, p. 24).

The interview protocol began with a short introduction and a verbal consent for videotaping followed by open-ended questions (Figure 3.1). Each ZOOM interview was videotaped and archived on my computer for transcribing. Every interview was conducted using the same questions from the protocol, but there were times when a follow-up question was asked or a probe for clarification or elaboration for a memory was requested. During each interview, I took field notes.

After each interview, a transcript of the interview was created. Transcription has always been a time-consuming process, but with the purchase of a new application, Otter.ai, it quickly produced a complete word-for-word transcript for each interview using the audio file of the video recordings. Each transcript identified both myself and the student for turns of talk and correctly inserted all punctuation. I was then able to convert the transcripts to .docx files.

Grounded Theory

After each interview was transcribed, the process of analysis begun. Using a grounded theory approach, I analyzed the data. Grounded theory is built upon the perspective that participants provide multiple realities (Charmaz, 2000) and the researcher creates links between these multiple realities. As an iterative process, in grounded theory, the researcher repeatedly returns to the data. Theory is then developed from the "categories that are systemically interrelated through statements of relationships" (Strauss and Corbin, 1998, p. 22). Thus, the researcher's theory is grounded in the interpretation of the data (Charmaz, 2006).

Glaser (1978 & 2002) has thoroughly outlined the steps for grounded theory methodology. Over time, other researchers, most notably Charmaz, have varied these steps, thus there is no one right way to conduct grounded theory. I used the process of open coding, then axial coding, and finally theoretical coding while also writing analytic memos throughout the coding process.

Retrospective Study ~ Thirteen Years Later
Interview Protocol

1. Opening
   It's so great to see you! I'm so happy you have agreed to participate in this interview. I want to remind you that you don't have to answer every question and you can end this interview at any time. I also want you to know that I am going to record this conversation. At the end of the study, I will delete all recordings. Do you understand? Do you have any questions about the study?

2. Background Information
   - Tell me how you are and what are you doing now.
   - Where did you go to high school?
   - Did you graduate? Regents diploma? Honors Regents?
   - What did you do after high school?
   - If college: What was your major? Why that major? Graduation?
     If no college: What kind of employment? Trade school?
   - Do you have any future plans/goals?

3. What do you remember about classroom talk during those three years we were together?

4. When I did my dissertation, I studied the classroom talk during our *Lunch is Gross* project.
   - Do you remember that project?
   - Have you ever thought or talked about that project since?
   - Did participating in that project have any influence on you? If so, in what ways?
   - Tell me how you use social media and for what purposes.
   - Tell me about any community groups with which you are involved.
   - Are you registered to vote? Do you vote in elections? If so, which ones?
   - Have you been involved in any pickets, protests, or projects that strive to make social change?

5. Is there anything else you remember about your second through fourth grade experience?

6. Closing
   Thank you so much for taking the time to talk with me. It was so great catching up with you and hearing your memories of our looped classroom.

Figure 3.1 Semi-Structured Interview Protocol

Open Coding

Beginning with an open coding process, the researcher initially enters the data through a line-by-line or word-by-word labeling of the data. This process allows the researcher to begin thinking about the data in relation to the experiences being examined. Charmaz suggests the following strategies for open coding:

- Breaking the data up into its component parts
- Defining the actions on which they rest
- Looking for tacit assumptions
- Explicating implicit actions and meanings
- Crystallizing the significance of points
- Comparing data with data
- Identifying gaps in the data

(p. 50)

The purpose of open coding is not to summarize or identify topics. Instead, open coding is to detect actions and processes, and to understand how the participants construct these actions and processes (Charmaz).

Open coding is the "pivotal link between collecting data and developing emergent theory to define what is happening in the data and ... to begin to grapple with what it means" (Charmaz, p. 46). Open coding is not done with any preconceived idea of codes; the codes develop directly from the data. Charmaz warns that the researcher's language is used to develop the codes and that includes all the biases, experiences, and understandings from that researcher. However, the process of constantly returning to the data in grounded theory helps the researcher to maintain the perspective of the study participants.

I began my open coding process by reformatting each interview. I copied and pasted the interview transcripts into a new Word document and numbered each line. Then I created a 5.5in margin on the right side of each page. I also used 3.0in spacing to have room for my line-by-line coding. I then coded every line by hand.

In order to code conceptually, it was important to use generalizable labels rather than descriptive ones. Therefore, I needed to avoid codes that would identify "time, place, and people" (Glaser, 2001, p. 10). Charmaz (2006) recommends using gerunds for the open coding process so as to "focus on actions and processes" for "seeing sequences and making connections" to go beyond the descriptive level (p. 136). A few of the codes I used were: feeling scared to speak; being in the news station; participating in something important; checking in with the teacher; and having expectations. As I coded every transcript line by line, reoccurring themes began to emerge. Some of these themes included: experiencing classroom activities, individualizing, learning outside the classroom, talking together, and having impact.

I also wrote analytic memos. These analytic memos recorded my thoughts and questions about the data. I repeatedly asked myself, "How does this connect to dialogic classrooms?" "What were the students remembering and what did it mean to them?" "What is the data telling me about dialogic classrooms?" "Are there patterns emerging?"

The last step of open coding is to identify categories from the themes. Identifying categories "are important for determining *what* is in the data" (Morse, 2008, p. 727). As I constantly compared the codes from the themes, I color coded the reoccurring words and ideas in order to begin to repeat words and information. The reoccurring words and ideas, along with the initial themes, were then collapsed categories. The three categories that emerged from the interview data included: relationships, social justice, and belonging.

Axial Coding

Open coding "fractures the data" into salient categories, while axial coding "begins to transform the basic data into more abstract concepts" (Tie, Birks & Francis, 2019). During the axial coding process, the researcher returns to the data to determine the properties and dimensions for each of the code categories identified (Strauss & Corbin, 1998). The axial coding process was highly detailed. Many researchers use qualitative data research analysis software; however, I like to sort the data strips on my large dining room table. I believe, as do Graue and Walsh (1998), that "handling the data gets additional data out of memory and into the record, which can "turn abstract information into concrete data" (p. 145).

I took each transcript and cut the line-by-line coding with the accompanying interview data into strips. These hundreds of strips were then sorted under one of the three code category headings. Once the raw data was sorted into the code categories, I then went back into each code category pile and resorted the strips to determine properties and dimensions. To discriminate and differentiate the properties and dimensions for each code category, I developed three concept maps.

Concept maps are a tool for diagramming and representing the relationships within code categories (Strauss & Corbin, 1998; Charmaz, 2006). Using my computer's Smart Art program, I developed a concept map for each of the three code categories. The concept maps created "a preliminary codebook – a predetermined set of constructs and their associated definitions and characteristics. This codebook will be refined throughout analysis" (Heydarian, 2016, para. 5). This third return to the data for resorting afforded me visual opportunities to compare data within the code categories.

Figure 3.2 illustrates one such concept map for the code category of "Belonging." Five major dimensions developed from the sorting process: Being a Family; Being a Team; Having Status; Feeling Pride; and Being Heard. Each of these dimensions were distinguished by properties using the students' words from the transcripts. The numbers following each property depict how many times it was mentioned in the interviews.

Throughout axial coding process, I continued to write analytic memos, considering the meaning of each students' words, and reflecting upon the students' memories. Once all properties were determined from the interview data, my attention shifted to developing theory to explain a retrospective view of a dialogic classroom.

Theoretical Coding

The theoretical coding procedure is designed to define and conceptualize the properties and dimensions of the code categories (Strauss & Corbin, 1994 & 1998). It is at this point that the researcher goes back into the data to make connections of the relevant data (Glaser & Holton, 2004) in order to descriptively elaborate, validate, and integrate the core categories. This directed and conceptual step of the analytic process provides a "check on the fit between the emerging theoretical framework and the empirical reality it explains" (Charmaz, 2000, p. 516) so that the researcher can begin to conceptualize how the code categories "may relate to each other as hypotheses to be integrated into a theory" (Charmaz, 2006, p. 63). This "involves the search for and identification of common threads that extend throughout an entire interview or set of interviews" (Morse & Field, 1995, p. 139) to determine an emergent theme.

Because I process and synthesize best through visual images, I created a visual representation (Figure 3.3) to examine the data for an emergent theme. Using this graphic enabled me to discover the dominant theme of identity.

The idea of identity in this case was to uncover what the reoccurring phrase "being an Explorer" meant to the students. Returning to the data once again, I selectively coded the data for the theme of identity. The process of selective coding was the first step in theorizing the concept of identity as it relates to the discursive pedagogy remembered by the Explorers.

Analytic Memos

Analytic memo writing occurs throughout the coding process. Memos are produced to record the researcher's thinking, which can be "both conscious and preconscious realizations as the research and the researcher grow"

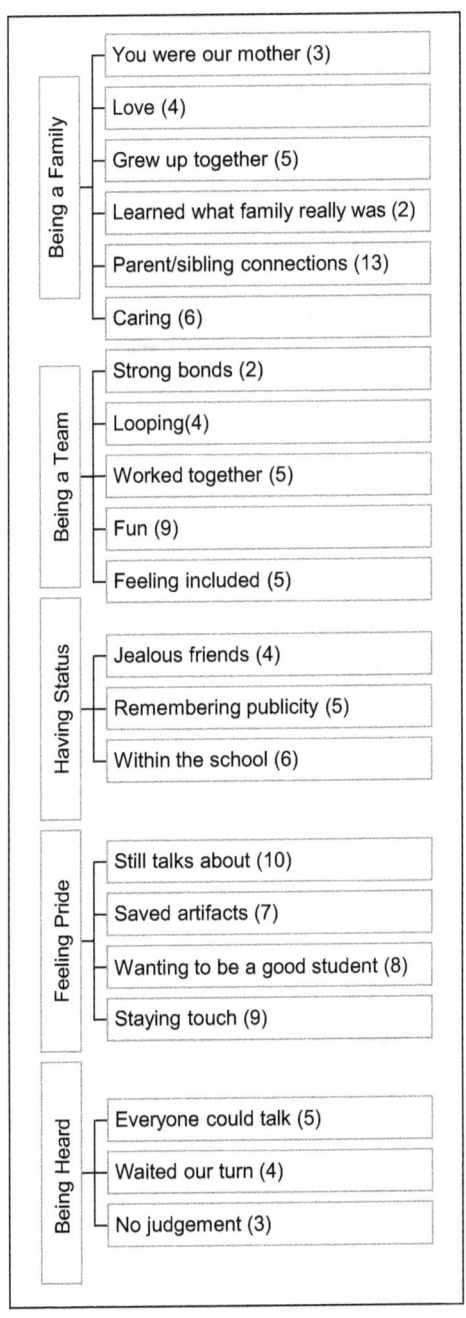

Figure 3.2 Axial Coding Process for the Code Category "Belonging"

52 *A Retrospective Case Study*

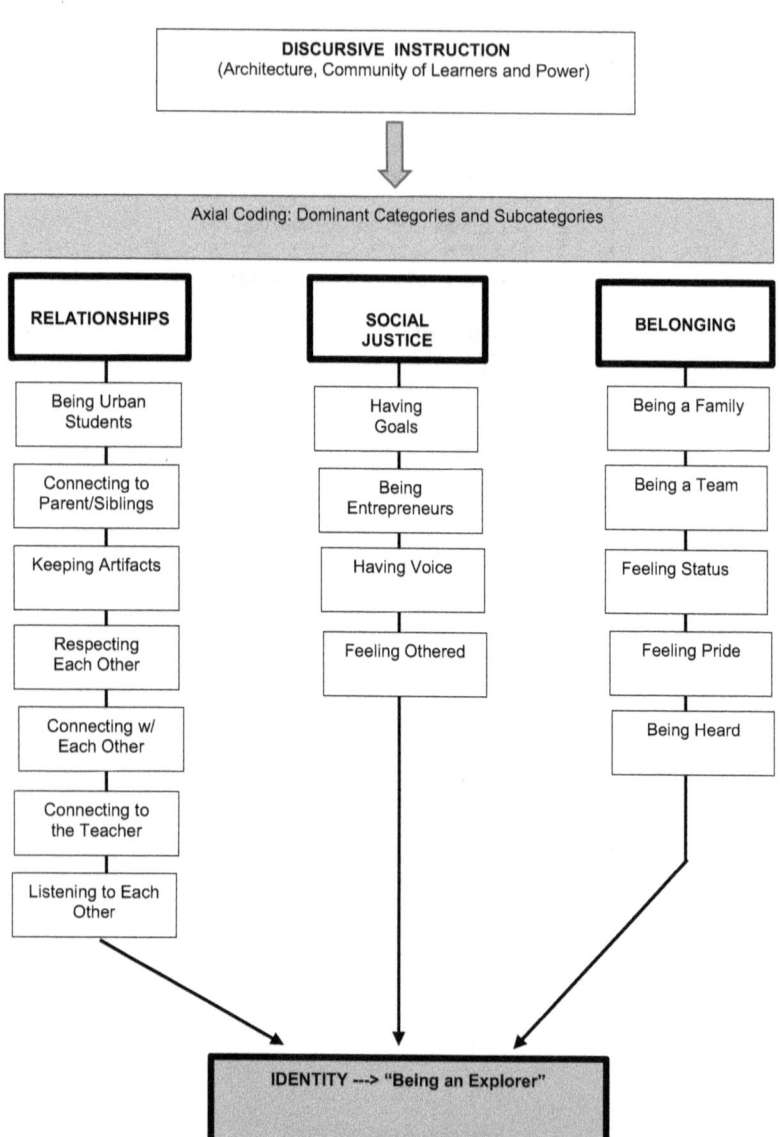

Figure 3.3 Visually Representing the Emergent Theme of Identity

(Glaser, 2013, Para. 6). The approach to writing memos is informal and personal. There are no rules for writing analytical memos. It is in memo writing where the researcher "forms the core of grounded theory" (Charmaz, 1996, p. 94). Strauss and Corbin (1998) advise researchers using grounded theory that, "if memos and diagrams are sparsely done, then the final product theory might lack conceptual density and integration" (p. 218).

I not only utilized many diagrams, but I also wrote memos throughout the coding and analytical process. An exemplar of one such analytic memo (Figure 3.4) demonstrates my thinking about the theme of identity when it initially emerged. This memo began with a list of the emerging categories and their characteristics. This was my first reflection of identity as an emergent theme from the category codes. Throughout the coding process, the memos became a place where I asked myself questions about the data, posed comparisons and dimensions for categories, and established theoretical possibilities. I also noted that I needed to read specific theorists to help me delve deeper into conceptualizing identity.

My memos, along with the visual representation of conceptualizing the categories and sub-categories for identity, were the first step in developing my grounded theory about identity as it relates to dialogic instruction. I continually returned to the data as a warrant for this emergent and developing theory. The empirically grounded data of the interview transcripts, analytic memos, diagrams, and concept maps ensured the voices of the students were considered and examined in the development of that theory.

Credibility of Grounded Theory

Detailing this iterative process of grounded theory is important. Qualitative researchers are often criticized for omitting their process of analysis and are therefore considered untrustworthy (Braun & Clarke, 2006), particularly those researchers using grounded theory (Suddaby, 2006). Thus, I have detailed my process of analysis in this chapter. However, it is not only important for the researcher to detail the systemic process for analysis, but also to discuss the researcher's constructs for interpretation.

Constructs for Interpretation

Peshkin (1988) defines subjectivity as the "amalgam of the persuasions that stem from the circumstances of one's class, statuses, and values interacting with the particulars of one's object of investigation" (p. 17). Denzin (1978) adds that subjectivity, in addition to personal beliefs, is also connected to the social and political environment at the time. Subjectivity is apparent in the choices researchers make in designing their study.

I'm about half way through open coding and I'm beginning to see some reoccurring categories emerge:
Comparisons
- to other classrooms
- urban/suburban schools

Relationships:
- students to students
- students to teacher
- parents/siblings to classroom
- Explorers to the school
- Explorers to the community/city

Real Life Experiences
- project going beyond school curriculum
- field experiences (hotels, restaurants, manners, fundraising)
- nursing home visits

Class Status
- within the school
- within their families
- as a past experience

Making Change
- choosing helping careers
- volunteering
- as Explorers

Caring Classroom
- respect
- self-esteem
- academic & emotional
- being heard

It seems as though identity has a connection to many of these. Identity plays a part in almost every one of these categories. The students identified as Explorers to their friends, families, and within the school. In many cases, this brough them a feeling of status, also us vs them mentality. Many of the students talked about themselves as change agents as Explorers and now as young adults either through their career choices, volunteering experiences, or through political activities. Almost every interview mentioned their long-term identification as an Explorer… "always will be an Explorer!" I was very surprised at the number of students that mentioned their commitment to schooling and doing well in school because they were Explorers. So many of the interviews mentioned their parents or siblings connected or identified as an Explorer too. Identity seems to take on multiple forms. I don't know much about identity theory. What are the ways identity is theorized? I think Gee has some work in identity theory. Check Lave & Wenger too. Who else? As I think about Gee's work, I wonder if the Explorers would be an affinity group rather than a community of learners? What exactly are the differences? Is it an either/or? I need to read more about this!

Figure 3.4 Analytic Memo Exemplar

It is through the lens of an urban teacher that I designed, analyzed, and interpreted my research. Given that most of my students were from non-dominant families living in poverty, issues of political, racial, economic, and power dynamics often impacted the teaching and learning in my classroom, especially within the dialogic interactions. It was the dialogic interactions that created spaces for exploring and acting upon racial, economic, and political issues that mattered to the students.

I approached this retrospective study contextualizing the experience of teaching the same class of elementary students over the course of three years, and clearly acknowledge that "the *way* in which we know is most assuredly tied up with both *what* we know and our *relationships with our research participants*" (Lincoln & Guba, 2000, p. 182). I have had a prolonged engagement with the students in this study. I was their teacher for three years and maintained a personal connection with most of the students for the subsequent thirteen years. I acknowledge my subjectivity throughout every chapter in this book, but my main objective is to accurately portray the voices of my students.

References

Abbot, S. & Cameron, S. (2020, November 4). *Engaging students as partners in learning and teaching: A retrospective.* [Blog post] Retrieved from www.centerforengagedlearning.org/engaging-students-as-partners-in-learning-and-teaching-a-retrospective.

Amir, P. & Amir, R. (1981). Retrospective curriculum retrospective: An approach to long-term effects. *Curriculum and Inquiry*, 11 (3), 259–278.

Anderson, D.J. (2009). *Systemic and personal change: A retrospective case study of balanced literacy implementation as perceived by those involved.* Unpublished dissertation. Retrieved from https://scholarworks.wmich.edu/dissertations/641.

Bogdan, R.C. & Biklen, S.K. (1992). *Qualitative research for education: An introduction to theory and methods.* Boston, MA: Allyn and Bacon.

Braun, V. & Clarke, V. (2006). Using thematic analysis in psychology. *Qualitative Research in Psychology*, 3 (2), 77–101.

Brock, C.H. & Wiest, L.R. (2012). A five year retrospective analysis of student learning in a university diversity course. *Journal of Higher Education Theory and Practice*, 12 (6), 59–73.

Charmaz, K. (1996). The search for meanings: Grounded theory. In J.A. Smith, R. Harre & L. Van Langenhove (Eds.), *Rethinking methods in psychology* (pp. 27–49). London, UK: Sage.

Charmaz, K. (2000). Grounded theory: Objectivist and constructionist methods. In N.K. Denzin & Y.S. Lincoln (Eds.), *The Sage handbook of qualitative research* (2nd ed., pp. 509–533). Thousand Oaks, CA: Sage Publications.

Charmaz, K. (2006). *Constructing grounded theory: A practical guide through qualitative analysis.* Thousand Oaks, CA: Sage Publications.

Conner, J.O. (2012). Ghosts of research past: Institutional memory and its implications for educational research. *International Journal of Research & Method in Education*, 35 (1), 93–104.

Denzin, N.K. (1978). *Sociological methods*. New York, NY: McGraw-Hill.

Galletta, A. (2013). *Mastering the semi-structured interview and beyond: From research design to analysis and publication*. New York, NY: New York University Press.

Gamble, M. (2007). *A retrospective study of the impact of a writing process program on the academic achievement of second, third, fourth, and fifth grade students*. Unpublished doctoral dissertations. San Francisco, CA: University of San Francisco.

Gersti-Pepin, C. (2002). Magnet schools: A retrospective case study of segregation. *High School Journal*, 85 (3), 47–52.

Glaser, B. (1978). *Theoretical sensitivity: Advances in methodology of grounded theory*. Mill Valley, CA: Sociology Press.

Glaser, B. (2001). *The grounded theory perspective: Conceptualization contrasted with description*. Mill Valley, CA: Sociology Press.

Glaser, B. (2002). Conceptualization: On theory and theorizing using grounded theory. *International Journal of Qualitative Methods*, 1 (2) 23–38.

Glaser, B. (2013). Introduction: Free style memoing. *Grounded Theory Review*, 2. Retrieved from http://groundedtheoryreview.com/2013/12/22/introduction-free-style-memoing/.

Glaser, B. & Holton, J. (2004). Remodeling grounded theory. *Forum Qualitative Social Research, 5 (2)*.

Golden, B. (1992). The past is the past–or is it? The use of retrospective accounts as indicators of past strategy. *The Academy of Management Journal*, 35 (4), 848–860.

Graue, M.E. & Walsh, D.J. (1998). *Studying children in context: Theories, methods, and ethics*. Thousand Oaks, CA: Sage Publications.

Hess, R.S. & Copeland, E.P. (2001). Students' stress, coping strategies, and school completion. *School Psychology Quarterly*, 16, 389–405.

Heydarian, N.M. (2016). Developing theory with the grounded theory approach and thematic analysis. *Association for Psychological Science*. Retrieved from www.psychologicalscience.org/observer/developing-theory-with-the-grounded-theory-approach-and-thematic-analysis.

Lincoln, Y.S. & Guba, E.G. (2000). Paradigmatic controversies, contradictions, and emerging confluences. In N.K. Denzin & Y.S. Lincoln (Eds.), *Handbook of qualitative research* (2nd ed., pp. 163–188). Thousand Oaks, CA: Sage Publications.

Morse, J.M. (2008). Confusing categories and themes. *Qualitative Health Research*, 8 (16), 727–723. Retrieved from https://journals.sagepub.com/doi/pdf/10.1177/1049732308314930.

Morse, M. & Field, A. (1995). *Qualitative research methods for health professionals*. Thousand Oaks: Sage Publications.

Peshkin, A. (1988). In search of subjectivity: One's own. *Educational Researcher*, 17 (7), 17–21.

Pozzi, D. & Lotyczewski, B.S. (2008). Preschool programming and its effectiveness. *Rochester Early Enhancement Project Retrospective Study Report*. Rochester, NY: Children's Institute. Retrieved from www.childrensinstitute.net/sites/default/files/documents/T07-006-REEP.pdf.

Rubin, H.J. & Rubin, I.S. (2012). *Qualitative interviewing: The Art of Hearing Data* (3rd ed.). Thousand Oaks, CA: Sage Publications.

Snipes, J.C. & Casserly, M.D. (2002). Urban school systems and urban reform: Key Lessons from a case study of large urban school systems. *Journal of Education for Students Placed at Risk*, 9 (2), 127–141.

Stake, R.E. (2000). Case studies. In N.K. Denzin & Y.S. Lincoln (Eds.), *Handbook of qualitative research* (pp. 435–453). Thousand Oaks, CA: Sage Publications.

Strauss, A. & Corbin, J. (1990). Grounded theory method: Procedures, canons, and evaluative criteria. *Qualitative Sociology*, 13, 3–21.

Strauss, A. & Corbin, J. (1998). *Basics of qualitative research: Grounded theory procedures and techniques*. Newbury Park, CA: Sage Publications.

Street, C. & Ward, K. (2012). Retrospective case study. In A.J. Mills, G. Durepos & E. Wiebe (Eds.), *Encyclopedia of case study research*. Thousand Oaks, CA: Sage Publications.

Strutz, M.L. (2012). A retrospective study of the elementary school experiences, influences, skills, and traits of talented engineers. *School of Engineering Education Graduate Student Series*, Paper 32. Retrieved from http://docs.lib.purdue.edu/enegs/32.

Suddaby, R. (2006). From the editors: What grounded theory is not. *Academy of Management Journal*, 49 (4), 633–642.

Tamir, P. & Amir, R. (1981). Retrospective curriculum evaluation: An approach to the evaluation of long term effects. *Curriculum Inquiry*, 11 (3), 259–278.

Tidwell, D. & Edwards, L. (2020). Retrospective self-study: Analysis of the impact of methods on thinking, teaching, and community. In C. Edge, A. Cameron-Standerford & B. Bergh (Eds.), *Textiles and tapestries: Self-study for envisioning new ways of knowing*. Retrieved from https://edtechbooks.org/textiles_tapestries_self_study/chapter_35.

Tie, C.T., Birks, B. & Francis, K. (2019). Grounded theory research: A design framework for novice researchers. *Sage Open Medicine*. Retrieved from https://journals.sagepub.com/doi/full/10.1177/2050312118822927.

Ufnar, J.A., Bolger, M. & Shepherd, V.L. (2017). A retrospective study of a scientist in the classroom partnership program. *Journal of Higher Education Outreach and Engagement*, 21 (3), 69–92.

Yin, R.K. (2003). *Case study research: Design and methods*. Thousand Oaks, CA: Sage Publications.

4 The Dialogic Classroom in Retrospect
Student Recollections and Long-Term Impacts

The Rochester City School District (RCSD) has been described as a high-poverty urban school district for over twenty years. During the time the Explorers entered the district as kindergarteners until the time they graduated, the city of Rochester consistently ranked high for childhood poverty among the nation's seventy-five largest metropolitan areas (Murphy, 2018). During those years, the RCSD had an 85% eligibility for free and reduced lunch, and the highest percentage of minority students of all urban school districts in New York State (NYSED, 2004–2016).

Between 2004 and 2016, the local newspapers and news stations did exposés on the challenges and failures of the Rochester City School District. Within those years, eight different superintendents administered the Rochester City School District's curricular and fiscal decisions. With each new superintendent, new visions and new innovations were instituted. District schools and central office staff were constantly being reorganized. Teacher morale was low and parents searched for alternatives. The number of charter schools began to grow.

This was also a time when curricular decisions were driven by high stakes testing. Prescriptive reading programs were purchased by the district and teachers were expected to use them, even if teachers had a track record of success with other approaches. Administrators began to surveil teachers for compliance of these scripted programs (Griffith, 2008). Teachers were singled out for not teaching beginning phonics, even if their students were reading at or above grade level. Test prep workbooks were purchased and teachers were expected to spend daily instructional time using them. In spite of these curricular priorities, the district test scores consistently ranked the lowest in state. By the time the Explorers graduated, the district's four-year graduation rate was 53%, with the drop-out rate being 31%.

In New York State, students graduate with either a Regents with Advanced Designation diploma, Regents diploma, or a Local Diploma. An Advanced Regents Designation requires passing eight Regents exams. Regents exams

DOI: 10.4324/9781003121893-4

are state standardized exams for high school core subjects. These exams are developed and administered by the New York State Education Department. A Regents diploma requires students to achieve a score of sixty five or higher on five Regents exams. These must include an ELA, math, science, and social studies exam along with one additional test in any of those areas. A Local diploma is an option designated for students identified with disabilities or for English Speakers of Other Languages (ESOL). They are only required to pass locally written final exams for each subject area.

The Explorers as a Cohort

The Rochester City School District (RCSD) collects their data for reporting to the state based on cohorts. These cohorts are not defined by grade level but instead by the year students enter ninth grade. Thus, the Explorers were part of the 2012 cohort, with the expectation that they would graduate in 2016. Every Explorer entered ninth grade in 2012. The RCSD data provided by the state for their cohort included a total of 2,097 students.

The racial make-up of this district cohort consisted of 59% Black, 26% Latinx, 11% Caucasian, and less than 4% Asian (data.nysed.gov). Of these students, 78% were identified as general education students, while 21% were students with disabilities, and 12% were ESOL. In comparison, the Explorers cohort was comprised of 52% Black, 28% Latinx, and 20% Caucasian. Special education services were received by 33% of the Explorers, while 23% received ESL services. Given the similarities of the district cohort to the Explorer cohort, the graduation outcomes would seemingly be comparable. However, that was not the case.

Outcomes for the 2012 Cohort

There were distinct differences in the graduation data between the district cohort and the Explorers' cohort, as depicted in Figure 4.1. The data for the district's 2012 cohort was collected from the New York State Education Department's website (NYSED, 2015–2016). Although only fifteen Explorers participated in the study, the graduation data for the class has been gathered for all twenty-one Explorers using district records. These graduation rates include all graduates as of August 2016.

The graduation rate for the Explorers was 32% higher than the district graduation rate. The percentage of Explorers awarded a Regents with Advanced Designation was 15% higher than the district percentage. The number of Regents diplomas awarded to the Explorers was 28% higher than the district cohort. While 12% of the district cohort students received local diplomas, no Explorer received a local diploma. The district cohort had

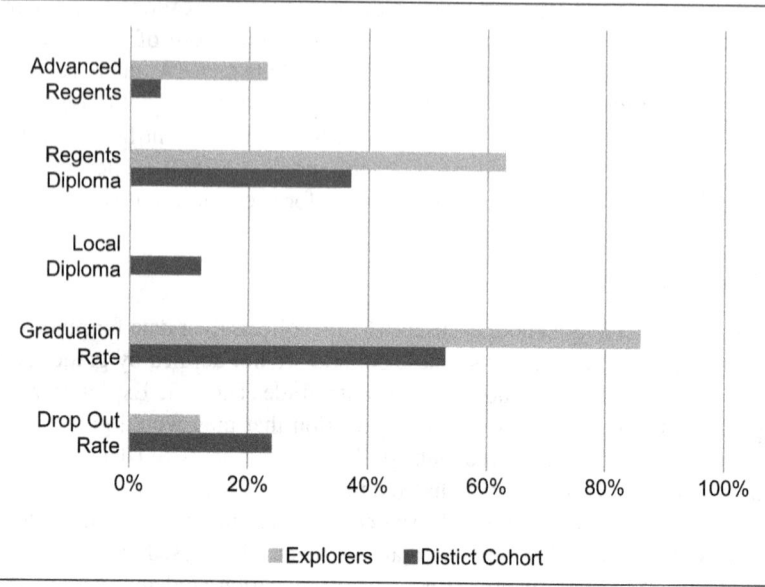

Figure 4.1 Graduation Data for RCSD 2012 Cohort

almost 20% more students than the Explorers drop out of school before high school graduation. These statistics do not include the additional 20% of district cohort students that stayed enrolled for a fifth year of high school. The graduation outcomes for those students are unknown. All of the Explorers graduated on time as four-year high school students. Of particular note, two Explorers were named as their class valedictorians. One of the valedictorians received ESOL services as an Explorer.

Rochester's Economic Context

In 2016, the year the Explorers graduated from high school, the unemployment rates were "astonishingly high" for high school graduates across the country (Kroeger, Cooke & Gould, 2016, section 2). For those projected to enter the workforce between 2016 and 2026, the employment market was dominated by jobs in the healthcare, construction, customer service, sales, and transportation fields as reported by the US Bureau of Labor (Torpey, 2018). These jobs are often hourly wages with little to no benefits. If, however, students continue their education and attain a college degree, they would be twice as likely to earn more money and live healthier lives (Hout,

2012). The income gap between those who attain a college degree and those that do not has widened in the 21st century and will continue to widen as the country's employment demand for skills in technology, science, engineering, and math increases (Gleeson, 2018).

In the last twenty years, mid-sized cities across the country, technology, and international competition replaced unskilled workers in US manufacturing jobs and factory work. This affected many urban cities, and particularly urban families. As a result, the rate of childhood poverty quickly increased. By 2010, almost 12 million children were living with food insecurity (Yu, Lombe & Nebbitt, 2010). Rochester, New York was one of those mid-sized cities, and the Explorers entered school during this time.

Between the time the Explorers began kindergarten (2004) and graduated high school (2016), Rochester's economic decline was steady. Rochester in the 20th century was a "boomtown," with Eastman Kodak, Xerox, and Bausch & Lomb employing about 60% of its citizens (Owens, 2018). There were other large manufacturers in Rochester that also provided job opportunities for unskilled or non-degreed workers. With just a high school diploma, folks in Rochester could make a decent living and have benefits. But, by the end of the 20th century, technological advances reduced the need for factory positions, and layoffs became the nightly news in Rochester. For twenty years, Eastman Kodak had large layoffs and finally, in 2012, declared bankruptcy. In that time, they went from 60,000 employees to 1,600. From 2008 to 2017, the poverty indicators confirm Rochester as one of the poorest mid-sized cities in the country (Murphy, 2018).

Although Rochester's job market has rebounded, the available positions are in the fields of engineering and information technology, for which college degrees or technical expertise are required. The manufacturing and production related positions require specialized training and at least a two-year degree. Additionally, the proximity to these available jobs shifted from cities to the suburbs, increasing the commute distance for urban residents (Kneebone & Holmes, 2015). The jobs available to high school graduates in Rochester are in retail, hospitality, and healthcare. These are minimum-wage jobs and offer less than forty hours a week with minimal or nonexistent benefits. The Explorers who chose to seek employment instead of higher education are having a difficult time earning enough to maintain a minimum standard of living.

Those Explorers who enrolled in college out of high school found the cost of attending college has never been higher (Clark, 2016). The high cost of a college education requires most students, especially those from low-income households, to borrow money to attend college. The number of students borrowing federal loans has more than doubled in the last ten years. Every Explorer who attended college financed their education through loans, both federal and private. Federal loans do not cover all of the expenses associated with attending college.

After High School for the Explorers

Every one of the fifteen Explorers interviewed for this study talked at length about the financial difficulties they are experiencing. Thirteen of the fifteen students interviewed enrolled in college after high school. Six enrolled in four-year colleges and the others enrolled in community colleges. Three students were awarded full-tuition scholarships. One student, who had a full tuition scholarship to a four-year college, expressed his gratitude, but "the loans for room and board, books, and fees were going to kill me." So, after his first semester, he decided to move home and transfer to the local community college.

Of the thirteen students that enrolled in college, five graduated on time. Two of them applied for and were accepted to graduate school. They both deferred enrollment due to the pandemic. They are both working and saving to pay for grad school. One of those that dropped out was a scholarship awardee. After three semesters, he was "overwhelmed" with how much debt he had incurred. Four students have dropped out of college. All four stated that, "College wasn't for me." The other four students have changed their enrollment status from full-time to part-time. They all mentioned the need to work while attending college.

Two students dropped out of the community college citing transportation issues. The local community college is located in a suburb of the city (although they have opened a downtown campus, not all courses are available there). One student explained, "I had to catch the bus seven blocks from my house and take it to the downtown terminal. Then, I had to transfer to another bus that took me out to the college. I was always late for class because the buses didn't run a lot. Once it got cold, it was awful. I finally just gave up; it was just too hard."

All but three of the Explorers live in Rochester and most I interviewed are living at home. They all talked about the high cost of housing "for crappy apartments." A few talked about not being able to get apartments because their credit scores are too low. Those working lamented that their employers do not give them enough hours to make any decent money. In most of the interviews, many spoke of their goals to "get out of Rochester" and the desire to "move somewhere nicer." They described Rochester as "bad" and having "too many people get shot." They all expressed dissatisfaction of the present-day Rochester and feeling that a move to another city would improve their satisfaction with life. Only one interviewee expressed a desire to move to Rochester's suburbs.

The Cohort's Study Participants

In the thirteen years since the Explorers went their separate ways, much has happened. Most recently, they have lived through political turmoil, racial tensions, and a global health pandemic. As they enter adulthood, I interviewed fifteen of the twenty-one Explorers. The following characterizations introduce the fifteen students interviewed for this study. Each narrative was constructed from my personal journal entries, my own memories, photographs, report cards, Facebook posts, and the interview transcripts. The students' names have been changed to ensure their anonymity.

Shamar

Once class rosters were released to faculty, the secretaries, administrators, and staff members voiced their sympathies about Shamar being on my class roster. I heard over and over, "he was the worst kid in the school." As I departed from my home visit, his father called after me, "good luck with him." During the first day of school, he made a very astute observation about the way a piece of equipment worked. He used highly scientific vocabulary and I wrote in my journal, "He may have been crawling on the rug while I was talking, but he was looking up into the overhead projector. He figured out how the overhead projector worked. He explained the light was refracting and reflecting off the mirrors. I think he's a smart boy, not a bad boy." I announced that Shamar would be our resident scientist. Although he was often out of his seat and loved to play tricks on the other kids and me, I quickly realized he was just avoiding the work. After a year of observing and collecting records, Shamar was evaluated and diagnosed with dysgraphia at the beginning of third grade. With differentiation of written activities and being in a classroom where he could share his knowledge orally, Shamar transformed into an engaged learner.

Upon high school graduation, Shamar attended a four-year historically Black college in another state. During his first year there, the college had significant financial problems and the cafeteria was closed. He "was hungry all the time," and he saw the school as "no different than my city high school." He returned home and transferred to a local community college which he attended for five semesters. He did not complete his program of study, citing the cost and the inability to pass two required classes. He now lives with family, works in a corporate warehouse as a union member, and exploring entrepreneurial possibilities.

Abigail

Abigail was one of a set of triplets and her mother described her as "the creative one," her sister as "the smart one," and her brother as the "athletic one." As a second grader, Abigail was timid and insecure. She would often cry at any task she felt was hard. She would cry when any project turned out less than perfect. When she cried, the other students would run to console her. She portrayed a sense of helplessness. But by the beginning of the second year, Abigail gained confidence as a learner. She cried less and became a comforter of other students instead of receiving comfort from them. She first discovered her voice through writing. She would beg for more time to write. Her creativity emerged first through writing, and then through the projects and classroom activities. Other students began to look to her for leadership. She was the student everyone wanted in their group for projects or activities. Once she gained confidence, she also became an active participant in all classroom discussions and felt very comfortable offering ideas or asking questions.

Abigail attended a four-year state college about an hour from her home. She graduated in four years majoring in technology management with a minor in culinary arts. After graduating college, she moved home and began working as a pastry chef in an area country club. She was saving money to "leave the country to learn more about baking," but the pandemic has stymied her travel plans. She continues to work as a pastry chef and will "hopefully travel soon." Eventually, she wants to open her own bakery.

Zahara

Zahara's mother had significant health problems, and although she wanted to participate in classroom activities, rarely could. Zahara often worried about her mother's health. Her mother confided in Zahara the details of her health and the difficulties of being a single mother. Her mother also relied on her to help at home, especially with her younger brother. As a result, Zahara was a mature student. Most of time she was happy, but some days she was quiet and sullen. She was kind and well-liked by the other Explorers.

Reading was Zahara's passion! She was an excellent reader and would have read all day if I let her. But she also eagerly participated in all activities and offered many of her thoughts to classroom conversations. Zahara was not only well read, but she also watched a lot of television at home. She was able to make connections between what she read, her own life experiences, and the current events of the city or country.

Zahara's mother passed away during her junior year of high school. She moved downstate to live with her aunt and graduated from a high school there. She enrolled as a performing arts major in a downstate community college. She works and attends college part time and still lives with her aunt. Her dream is to "move to California and begin a singing career."

Blakely

Blakely was serious child. As a second grader, she worked hard and was rather quiet. But upon returning to third grade, she emerged from her subdued ways and became very involved in all classroom activities. She often found a quiet place to work without interruptions. She excelled at making conceptual connections, especially in reading and writing.

Blakely was always very careful about the way she said things. She never wanted to offend or hurt anyone's feelings. She was a respected member of the class. When Blakely spoke, everyone listened. By the end of fourth grade, Blakely was an avid reader and writer, but also excelled in mathematics.

Blakely graduated high school with college credits. She attended a local four-year state college majoring in pre-law. She completed her four-year degree while working part-time. She is currently working full-time as a home healthcare worker and living at home. She requests as much over time as possible in order to earn enough money to attend law school full time in the near future. She plans to become a lawyer "who will provide legal services for families living in poverty."

Farrah

On the first day of school, Farrah announced her entrance, and then she never stopped talking for the entire three years! She was smart, funny, and engaging, but demanded attention. She enthusiastically participated in every activity. Farrah always had something to offer to any conversation. As a second grader, she constantly interrupted other speakers, but by the end of fourth grade, she developed better listening skills and, for the most part, respectfully waited her turn.

Farrah was quick to learn new concepts. She asked good questions and offered important points, but they sometimes got lost in her constant need to talk. The special subject, teachers complained to me about her. They often sent her to the office for talking out of turn or interrupting the teacher.

After high school graduation, Farrah attended one semester of community college and realized that college was "not for me." So she began her career as an exotic dancer because "the money is great and I get to travel." She performs at a local club and for private events all over the country. Once she's "too old" to perform, she plans to go to cosmetology school so she can open her own business.

Brandi

Brandi was a sweet, shy little girl when she entered second grade. She was timidly compliant. Her parents were involved and active in school events and classroom activities. Her mother brought her to the classroom door every morning. She often donated to our snack basket. Her father worked in the mailroom at the district's central office and each year, when we held a wreath sale to raise funds, he assisted us in the delivery of the more than a hundred wreaths ordered by the central office staff.

By the time Brandi was a fourth grader, she was no longer a quiet, shy, or timid. She was keen to participate in all classroom activities and spoke up often. She was an average student and often looked to the other girls for validation, both academically and socially.

Brandi majored in psychology at a four-year college about two hours outside of Rochester. She graduated on time and has been accepted to a master's program for school counseling in a university in a nearby city. She moved home and is employed as a behavioral technician in a program for autistic children. After she attains her master's degree, she plans to work in a school setting where she can " help kids through tough situations."

Celina

Celina was a petite, adorable little girl. She was the princess of her family and came to school in trendy outfits every day. She was bilingual and would sometimes confuse English with Spanish. Her mother and father were active in classroom activities and would often bring other family. They were very proud of everything Celina did.

As a student, she was energetic and interested in all that we did. Her participation in classroom discussions was always enthusiastic and very respectful. But Celina's contributions to classroom discussions were mostly repetition of what others had offered. Celina was mostly interested in the social aspect of the classroom interactions. By fourth grade, Celina was often in the middle of any boyfriend/girlfriend drama.

After high school graduation, Celina worked full-time in retail and attended the local community college as a part-time student. In her first semester, Celina became pregnant and "couldn't do it all." She felt she "wasn't ready for college" and "didn't really know what to major in," so she dropped out. At that same time, she was offered a position with a company in sales to represent products for skin care, hair care, and cosmetics. She has been successful at this job and it's something she "loves to do every day!"

King

King entered second grade as a silent student; he refused to speak. He would communicate by using gestures, facial expressions, or nodding. He was mild mannered and would speak to a few of the other students, but only in whispers. His mother informed me that he spoke at home but had no idea why he refused to speak in school. His selective mutism did not interfere with his academic performance. In fact, he was a good student. With much positive reinforcement and encouragement, King slowly began to speak during classroom activities. By the end of fourth grade, he was no longer a selective mute.

King was especially astute in math and science. He grasped new math practices quickly and was always the first one to finish a math assignment. Many student in the class would ask him for help in math. Many requested him as a partner for any science project.

As a Rochester Scholar, a scholarship program for all Rochester City School District students who were accepted to local four-year colleges, King attended a local institution as a computer technology major. He loved being on the campus and being immersed in college life. But he had "one night of stupidity" and got a girl pregnant. He is committed to co-parenting his son. He is majoring in computer sciences and hopes to secure a programming position with a large company.

Alena

Alena's mother moved her to Rochester from New Jersey the summer before second grade began. When I made a home visit, Alena's mother only spoke Spanish, so Alena translated for her mother. They moved to Rochester to be near a distant relative. But after a few months, they stopped speaking. Alena and her mother were alone in a new city. Alena's mother had no car and no job. They did connect with a local church who helped them.

As an ESOL student, Alena struggled with reading and writing. She was serious about learning and worked hard. She never hesitated to ask for help from the other students or me. Alena was proficient enough to have conversations in English. She contributed much to our classroom conversations.

As a high school junior, Alena and her mother moved back to New Jersey. Alena applied for and was accepted to a pre-military program, but she accidently became pregnant, and had to drop out of the program. She cried as she explained, "I had so many plans. I wanted to be a social worker." As a single mother she spends all of her time with her son or at work. She is in a training management program for a fast food chain. She told me, "I hate it, but it's what I have to do for my son." Her mother lives with her and provides care for her son while she is at work. She attends a GED program but is not sure when she will take the exam.

Luca

Transferring from a charter school, Luca entered our classroom as a very timid and compliant child. He was virtually a non-reader, and was repeating the second grade. He often referred to himself as "dumb." But he worked hard and his parents asked for advice on supporting him at home. He began to make steady progress.

By the beginning of third grade, Luca was a different child. He seemed happy and confident. His confidence soared, and he began to take academic risks. He also started to display a sense of humor. He would crack jokes and even laugh at himself when he made mistakes. He was a well-liked member of the class.

Luca graduated high school and entered the community college's mechanics technician program as a continuation to the vocational coursework he completed as a senior in high school. He "was good at math and wanted to be an engineer," but college was too expensive and he "had to contribute to the family." He lives at home and works at a local auto dealership as an entry-level technician. When the coursework went online due to COVID, he took a leave of absence because he "couldn't focus with online courses." He assured me that, "as soon as they go back to face to face" he'll finish the two classes he has left for his associate's degree. He "hopes to travel as much as possible."

Travion

Travion was not on my original class roster; instead, he was repeating first grade. After three weeks of school, I was called to a meeting with the principal, vice principal, and school psychologist. They explained that Travion's first grade teacher was having a very difficult time handling him and they felt it would be best for him to move to second grade. That afternoon, he was moved to our class.

Travion had a significant learning disability and had been diagnosed with ADHD by his pediatrician. When Travion entered our classroom, he was in the middle of a prescription trial for ADHD. His mother resisted the medication, but agreed to the trial. Travion had severe headaches and slept through much of the day during that trial. Even adjusting the medication dosage had little positive results. Ultimately, she chose not to medicate him.

Travion talked constantly and loudly. His behavior and response to others was impulsive. He could only read three words ("I," "and," and "the"). His special education services were scheduled for one hour a day, but he often refused to go. His mother and father were very involved parents. In fact, his father camped out with us every year and his mother came on most field experiences. Over the three years as an Explorer, Travion became a functional reader and improved his impulse control.

As a high school student, Travion was a star basketball and football player, but his grades left him sidelined for sports his senior year. He dropped out of high school and sold marijuana. He has been arrested as a low-level drug dealer and for battery and assault. He has spent time in and out of prison. He has a daughter, and when not in prison, he lives with his girlfriend and is a stay-at-home father. His girlfriend works full-time.

Bria

Bria's family immigrated from an eastern European country. I taught her two older sisters and when I made a home visit before Bria entered my classroom, her mother insisted I stay for dinner. Her mother spoke very little English, so Bria and her sisters translated. Her parents did not participate in any school activities, but made sure Bria participated every event connected to our classroom. Bria loved to stay after school to help me and her parents would allow her, provided I would drive her home.

Bria was an outgoing and caring student. She was friends with everyone and never had a negative interaction with any other student the entire three years as an Explorer. She was not only an outstanding student in every subject, but also very creative. Her ability to draw made her a popular illustrator for any project and her classmates' published stories.

Although Bria was her class valedictorian, she did not apply to college. Instead, she took a gap year. She traveled to her home country to visit family and travel throughout Europe for a year. Upon her return home, she entered a four-year college as an accounting major. She lives at home and will be graduating with a bachelor's degree on time. Her future plans include working for a large company and traveling as much as possible.

Keagan

Keagan's family also immigrated from the same eastern European country as Bria's. Their families were friends. His mother was very involved in school activities and often delivered her homemade baklava as a class treat. Everything stopped when she arrived unannounced carrying a large tray. Keagan received support from an ESOL teacher until high school.

Keagan was a very quiet and compliant student. He was excellent math student. He read and wrote with little difficulty, but he lacked confidence. He listened intently but rarely participated in classroom discussions. If he was in a small group with his small circle of friends, he would become animated and involved. Otherwise, he would passively participate.

Keagan graduated high school and entered the local community college. He attended part-time, majoring in health administration. He lives at home and assists in his mother's cleaning business. He spends much of his free time playing computer games. During his ZOOM interview, I noticed and commented on the three computer screens I saw in the background. He told me that he built two of them. He needs to complete one more class for his associate's degree and plans to transfer to a local college to complete his bachelor's degree. He hopes to attend full-time but "his mother may need him to keep helping with her cleaning business."

Alexa

Over the three years Alexa was an Explorer, I never met her mother. My six attempts to make a home visit were met with cancelled appointments or an unanswered door. I did speak with her mother a few times by phone. Her mother never participated in any classroom activities. She did, however, make sure Alexa attended all classroom activities.

As an Explorer, Alexa liked to read and would often talk about the books she was reading. She liked any group project and would enthusiastically participate in those. She had the potential to be a good student, but really only cared about the social aspects of school. She did participate in classroom discussions, but infrequently. She would be the one student who consistently initiated sidebar social conversations. Most of the time, the other students would shush her and she would get mad and sit sullenly. If there was an argument or drama, Alexa was involved.

Alexa graduated high school and immediately entered the workforce. She worked retail and quickly rented her own apartment. While working, Alexa attended a training program for cosmetology and received her state license. She has recently opened her own extension lash business in a corner of her apartment where she displays product and offers services. She continues to work retail while she "builds her clientele." She considers her lash business a second job at the moment, but stives to open her own shop and "be her own boss."

Seth

Seth was an only child. He and his mother lived with his grandmother. The grandmother dominated the conversation during the home visit. She wanted to make sure I knew how smart Seth was and wanted to know how I was going to challenge him. During second grade, his grandmother would deliver him to the classroom and loudly complain about the previous day's events. She would perceive Seth's retelling of an event as unfair treatment or "not good education."

Seth was an excellent reader and learned new skills quickly. He was a fount of knowledge. In fact, he was like a walking encyclopedia. At first he had a great deal of difficulty being in an inquiry-based classroom; he valued facts as learning, not investigation and explanation. Although Seth worked cooperatively with everyone, his demeanor was always that of a loner. His social interactions were only with two other boys in the class for the entire three years.

Seth was his senior class valedictorian. He attended a local four-year college and majored in computer science. He was awarded a significant scholarship. He lived on campus and admittedly had a hard time adjusting to college life. He dropped out and moved down south near relatives. He is working on a Mississippi riverboat.

The Explorers Reflect Retrospectively

Each interview elicited memories of being an Explorer. One student said what so many others did, "There is a lot to remember!" Before she was even asked about her memories of being an Explorer, Zahara made the statement, "I remember a lot! We did so much!" Blakely shared that "even after thirteen years," she "still tells her friends about being an Explorer." As soon as Farrah's image appeared on the computer screen, she provided a rendition of the ritual chant that signaled the start of reading each day.

The fifteen students interviewed were eager to think back to their experience as an Explorer. Their many memories reflected five themes. These themes included: experiencing classroom activities, individualizing, learning outside the classroom, talking together, and having impact.

Experiencing Classroom Activities

When I referenced the *Lunch is Gross* project during the interviews, every student had vivid recollections. King explained the project as he remembered it. "It was real research. Not just looking something up on the internet. We conducted surveys, and found menus from the suburban schools to see what those kids ate for lunch." Other aspects of the project were remembered, such as interviewing adults, videotaping in the lunchroom, creating fruit and vegetable costumes and wearing them to parade in front of the camera, writing a script, producing a documentary, and going to the Board of Education to picket. In her interview, Brandi described Seth's healthy food costume, "Remember how we tied those purple balloons all around him to be grapes?" Blakely told me she has the video bookmarked on her computer and shows her friends, "even just a few months ago." Zahara shared that she took a science of food class in college and asked the professor if she could show the class the video. She said the professor and the class "were really impressed." Brandi also mentioned the video in her psychology class when they were studying health and coping. The professor immediately pulled up the video and her class watched it. She reported, "they thought it was so cool."

As they reminisced about the *Lunch is Gross* project, they also referenced other classroom projects and activities. One student declared, "There were just so many!" And Farrah remembered that "everything was so creative." Multiple interviews referenced the electrifying of the mini houses. Others mentioned maintaining the walk-in butterfly vivarium they had inherited from the previous cohort. They remembered turning the vivarium's PVC pipe structure into an ocean museum, a longhouse, and finally an aviary. They also recalled publishing the Whale magazine, turning the classroom into a dinosaur museum ("with the smoke machine for the walk through volcano") and "putting up that greenhouse and working in the garden every Tuesday." Luca even remembered the very first project completed by the Explorers during the opening week of second grade. He told me, "I still have the Family Box, you know, where we had to introduce ourselves to everyone else through a box of pictures and stuff we brought in."

"It was all so hands-on," was how Alexa described the classroom learning. Keagan talked about how he "got a bad grade in math" when in first grade. But "after playing all the math games and hands-on activities for math" as an Explorer, "I became really good in math." Every single interview described the projects and activities as "fun." Travion expressed what many others said: "We were learning, but it was so much fun!" Another student summarized the learning in the classroom as, "It was never JUST fun, but instead, it was fun to LEARN!"

In most of the interviews, the students remembered the classroom's physical space. "It wasn't like any other classroom in the school, and I've never seen another classroom like it," was how King recalled it. Blakely described the classroom as "sectioned off for different reasons," and Abigail spoke of "the spaces in the room with a ton of stuff and a ton to do." One student described the room in great detail. "One corner of the room was for the computers and then there was a book corner. The book corner had a rug. We had so many books to choose from. The hamster was there on a bookshelf. We had pillows and bean bag chairs to sit on. And, if we were reading silently we could go over there to read or take the pillows or bean bags to another place in the room."

Brandi remembered the office alcove where a wall phone hung above the desk. She remembered how, "she always liked to sit there to do her work when she wanted quiet." Abigail also remembered the "office area," but her memory focused on how the students were taught to answer the phone and take a message. She commented, "I still answer the telephone the way you taught us to, 'Hello, this is Abigail, how may I help you?'"

Celina was the only one who remembered the "snack basket," where anyone could get a package of crackers when they were hungry. But every Explorer remembered the many animals. "We had so many pets" was repeatedly stated throughout the interviews. Alexa remembered, "We had to take care of them." The hissing cockroaches, gerbils ("remember how the gerbils kept having babies?"), turtles, fish, crabs, and the tarantula were all named. But the snake evoked strong memories. In one interview, with a raised voice, Farrah recalled, "I remember I had to sit next to the snake cage, and even though it had a padlock on it, it still freaked me out!"

As she recalled the classroom projects, Blakely reflected, "we learned so many new things." Towards the end of her interview, Abigail stated, "It just didn't seem like a classroom." "We did things out of the box," summed up one student, and another declared, "Learning was an adventure for those three years."

Individualizing

Some of the Explorers felt that in this classroom their own individuality mattered. As Shamar remembered the many classroom experiences, he recalled Spotlight on the Author. He reminisced, "Whoever was under the spotlight, got the attention of everyone. Even though I hated to write, I wrote because I remember feeling really good when I got out from under the spotlight." He also remarked, "During SSR (silent sustained reading) I was allowed to lay on the floor under the computer shelf or under my desk where I was comfortable. You didn't care as long as I was reading."

Seth recalled his contribution to the dinosaur museum: "I was totally into the computer and only wanted to participate if I could do something on the computer." He then elaborated, "You taught me to use the program for the clicker system and I made a quiz for the visitors to take at the end of their museum tour [and] that the kids in the other classes could take when they visited the museum. I remember I tried to write hard questions and trick them. I spent the whole day at the clicker station. I really loved it!"

In her interview, Alena brought up her difficulty with English but said, she "never felt bad about it" because, "you and me were really close. You were patient and taught me the words I didn't know." Keagan spoke of learning English as "barriers" throughout his education. "No one ever made fun of my accent," he noted. He reminded me that I helped him with his writing, especially with "using the right words, verb tenses, and that."

Keagan also cited his religion, which forbade him to participate in any holiday celebrations as making him feel different from the other students.

He remembered, "You had us do Explorer Friendship Day instead of Valentine's Day. We had to do something nice for someone else in the class. Then, we had a party. You never had any holiday parties, so I never felt left out." Bria too, who also didn't celebrate holidays, spoke about how glad she was that we never celebrated holidays as class events. That way she "didn't have to be sent to the office to sit out during the holiday parties," as she did in the classrooms before and after being an Explorer.

A few students talked about their home lives and how the home visits I made before the beginning of second grade were important. "You knew about us," said one student. Luca brought up the home visits and reflected, "I think the home visits were a way for you to gauge what each of us were like and how we learned. I think that made a huge difference, in terms of relating to us and knowing a little bit about each one of us." He viewed the home visits as a way for me to, "Learn some little things about each one of us to get to know us individually." Luca correlated the home visits to individualized instruction. "You know how they say people learn differently? Well, you always encompassed every single learning style, in some sort of way in each lesson that you taught. And then we practiced, and for those that didn't get it, you always went one on one with them." He reiterated, " If we didn't get it one way, then you found another way to teach it, so we did get it."

Learning Outside the Classroom

Integral to what was being taught in the classroom were field experiences. Whenever we left the classroom to go out into "the real world," I would remind them, "This is not a vacation! This is a learning experience!" Alena excitedly reminisced, "Those field trips were awesome! Not only were they a learning adventure, but we had so much fun at the same time. It was like school and life experience put together." Another student remembered them as " fun trips but always educational."

The school district did not fund field experiences. I felt it was unreasonable to ask parents, many who were living at or below the poverty level, to pay for these supplemental experiences. So, whenever a grant or funding opportunity became available, I would apply. I approached corporations and local businesses to secure financing or donations of goods. But I also had the students raise funds for the expenses. Each year, we raised funds through entrepreneurial endeavors. Our yearly wreath company was by far the most lucrative fundraiser. We had repeat customers every year and had profits well over a $1,500. We also had a Mother's Day Flower sale, Birthday card company, and CandyGrams for Valentine's Day. One time, at the suggestion of a student, we sold copies of our Whale magazine at lunch time. We sold out in one day and netted $150. Each of these enterprises involved writing, communication, and mathematics. "Those sales really helped us learn about money," one student declared. Another remembered, "our parents actually put the responsibility on us too. We had to sell all that stuff ourselves. We got so good at selling." Travion declared, "We really made a lot of money in those three years!"

At the end of each year, we took overnight trips. At the end of second grade, we did a one-night trip, then for the third grade trip we went a little further and stayed two nights. To culminate our three years together, we took a three-night trip. These overnight trips involved hours-long bus trips. We made stops along the way for sightseeing, park visits, and tours. On the bus ride, they used road maps to follow the route, wrote in their journey diaries, and even read silently. Once we arrived at our destination, there was always a dining and hotel experience. One student recalled, "We went on so many trips. The overnight ones were the best. . . . Williamsburg, Hershey, Albany. And I loved how someone's parent stayed in our room with us; we had so much fun!" Bria told me that she still has the framed picture published in the *New York State Conservationist* (my husband sent it into the newspaper). She caught a huge fish as we stopped to hike and fish in our three-day journey along the Hudson River. On that same trip, we stopped in Albany and Abigail remembered meeting with our state senator. She remembered asking him why they had to hear "gun shots at night in their neighborhoods."

But there were many other field experiences, as well. "We went camping! What class goes camping?" exclaimed one student. Another remembered an overnight the first week of school in the gym. It was their very first field experience of second grade. For Keagan, the highlight of that experience was when my husband brought in his twenty-foot python. "We still have pictures of the entire classroom lined up in the gym with a giant snake." His mother brought in a snack for the class and his younger brother accompanied her. "He was at the very end of the snake and he had the snake's tail wrapped all around him. My mom still talks about that."

Blakely remembered the monthly field experiences we took to the nursing home and how we did craft projects with "patients that had no families to visit them." Alexa ticked off the field experiences she remembered, "The Magical Mystery scavenger hunt every year, instead of celebrating birthdays, where we ended up in the bakery or the pizza place; the plant conservatory; Channel Eight News station; camping; every museum in Rochester; Ellison Park; and Charlotte Beach."

Students compared their high school trips to the trips they took as Explorers. One explained, "We actually went to Hershey Park for my band trip, and when we got there, I thought, 'Oh yeh, I've already been here, I've done that.'" Brandy described how she and Abigail were on a high school trip to Washington, DC and they felt as though they "had a leg up on the others." She reminisced, "We told everybody how we went on all these overnight trips in elementary school." Then she reflected, "the high school trip was just a different kind of experience. We just went [and] walked around museums the whole time. It wasn't memorable. It wasn't fun."

Talking Together

One of the interview questions asked the students, "what do you remember about how classroom talk occurred?" When Zahara was asked this question, she responded with an itemized accounting:

- We were able to be open.
- We could say anything.
- We could speak our minds.
- We weren't judged.
- We were allowed to communicate with each other.
- We voiced how we felt to each other.
- We could open up to each other.

Others remembered the classroom talk as discussing things together. Bria spoke of being able to talk to each other during independent work times. She remembered how other students would come to her for help and she would "never give them an answer but just help them find the answer." Alexa remembered that she "was always coming up with creative ideas to do reading projects" and "you let me change the way to do them."

Many of the interviews connected the physical environment in relation to the classroom talk. "I remember talking a lot on the rug during read aloud," said one student. Four students mentioned the arrangement of the desks as influencing classroom talk. King reflected on the student desks forming a large rectangle as, "We didn't look at the back of someone's head. We sat face to face and everyone could see and hear what each other was saying." Brandi paralleled King's explanation: "We could see everybody's faces, like nobody's back was to us because we wanted to see everybody being able to speak and hear everybody's point of view."

Shamar seemed to have a distinct memory for the way in which talk occurred. "We didn't have to raise our hands. We didn't talk over each other, we just waited for our turn. We had mutual respect for each other. If you didn't agree with someone, it was expected that you would respect their opinion. If someone had a question or didn't understand, then we didn't move on until the person fully understood." It was evident the Farrah also had as strong memory of classroom talk. She remembered, "I talked a lot. I used to interrupt people and you would remind me that I had to give other people a chance to talk. I learned to let other people think through their thoughts, and that everyone should have a turn."

"You talked with us, not at us," was the way Michelle remembered the classroom talk. Thinking back, Seth explained, "we talked to everyone, not just you. Everyone paid attention to whoever was talking. It was a group conversation." Alexa described to me that, "you would ask a question and then we would talk. You allowed us to talk to each other. You taught us not to be afraid to speak up." Even though Keagan seldom spoke during classroom conversations, he remembered that, "We took our turns talking. We would end up trying not to overlap each other. No [one] felt left out, you know?" Seth described the classroom talk as improving his self-esteem. "I didn't want to talk, it was outside of my comfort zone, but I wanted to be heard, so I broke out of my shell."

Five students mentioned that they never had another class where the teacher let the students talk. Blakely remembered that the field experiences and the classroom afforded opportunities to "talk to each other about what we were learning." When Abigail considered her answer to the question about the classroom talk, she concluded, "The Explorers, we had voice. I never had another class, not even in college, where we were allowed to talk. The teacher always led the discussion."

Having Impact

After spending three years together, from second to fourth grade, the Explorers were divided among four fifth grade classrooms. Although never asked about it, five students brought up the distinct difference of moving up to fifth grade. One student told me, "It very hard for all of us to kind of comprehend that we were no longer going to have that (being an Explorer)." Another student explained that moving onto fifth grade meant, "I had to get used to sticking to the teacher's plan, all the time, the students didn't matter." "It was a drastic change," said another. One student described the transition to fifth grade as "completely different; it was just insane." "But we got used to it," Alena explained.

Once in secondary school, the twenty-one Explorers were scattered among the district's nineteen secondary schools and charter schools. One student was enrolled in the urban-suburban program. This program bussed out students to a suburban school from the city. King explained his secondary experience as feeling "shocked at how little people knew and how they acted. One girl even told me, 'Why do you talk like a white person?'" To which he declared to me, "I talked like that because as an Explorer I learned to be educated." He went on explain that being an Explorer impacted him as a college student. He told me:

> My capstone project for my Associates degree is on human trafficking and I think the research we did for Lunch is Gross made me believe I could change things in the world, to make things better. We all saw what we could do as fourth graders. When I see those milk cartons with the missing children pictures, I think, I can do better. I want to create a LogRhythm for a mapping program of missing children. Being an Explorer made me believe in myself.

Luca also felt that being an Explorer positively impacted his secondary school success. "I mean honestly, like I think I wouldn't be the person I am today if I didn't have the learning I did as an Explorer," he explained. He felt that he would "have never learned to read and catch up" if he hadn't been an Explorer. Zahara also credits being an Explorer for her school success. She said, "I would think so many times in high school, and even in some college classes, 'I already learned this when I was an Explorer.' I gained confidence as a learner"

The question of impact evoked a strong response from Blakely: "I'm in college and that has everything to do with being an Explorer. I would have never stayed in school. I learned to love learning and school because I was an Explorer." Shamar, too, had deep emotions about being an Explorer: "Everything important in life, I learned in that classroom. I wanted to be there every day. It made us all want to be good students."

Some of the Explorers felt their three-year experience impacted their choices for careers. Brandi felt as though she "found herself" as an Explorer. "I hated all the talking in second grade but I made myself talk. I wanted to be part of it all," she remembered. Having "a voice" in that classroom, "It helped me to find myself," she reflected. " I just loved being in school as an Explorer and that's when I decided I want to work in a school. I thought I wanted to be a teacher but realized that wasn't for me, so now I'm going to be a school counselor." Keagan succinctly replied, "Obviously being an Explorer impacted me. I'm trying to make something of myself."

Celina spoke extensively about how the *Lunch is Gross* project "especially" taught her to "stand up for what I believe in." She articulated:

> We were so passionate about how our school food sucked. We knew the way the food should look like, and the freshness of it, and the quality of it. When we protested in front of the Board of Education, that's when I realized that I have to fight for something I want. That is something I

do every day now. Sometimes my job is hard and I want to give up but I remember that little girl that believed. I still have that in me.

During the interviews, many of the students spoke of the desire to travel as a result of the Explorers traveling out of state. Farrah has the desire to travel like that again so she can "stay in fancy hotels" and "eat in real restaurants." In six of the interviews, a desire to "see the world" or "travel as much as I can" was expressed. Bria told me that as she traveled around Europe during her gap year, she thought about "all the traveling we did as Explorers, and the trips you took with your husband." Three other Explorers have also traveled to countries outside the United States.

It was notable how many Explorers are presently involved in social justice efforts. Shamar watches the news "all the time" and spends his free time writing and producing "songs about bettering yourself, living in poverty, and having morals." He writes from his " Black point of view of the world." He posts his songs to social media. Abigail was president of her service sorority in college and now volunteers as an assistant Girl Scout leader. She led the fight against her college taking over the student development space. Zahara has a body positivity blog and she was part of an organization that successfully petitioned for gender-neutral bathrooms. Celina has become a vegan because she "can't take the cruelty to animals." As a "mixed race" kid, Brandi described racist occurrences at her college. "So, a group of us made our voices heard. We made significant change. We helped organize three new clubs on the campus (Black Lives Matter, LGBTQ, and Asian). I was vice president of the Black Lives Matter club." Blakely volunteers at a law firm that provides free legal services to low-income individuals. She conducts intake interviews of many homeless and mental health patients. "It's very, very emotional." Although King doesn't care about national politics, he is interested and participates in local politics because "that's what really counts for my life." Although he is sympathetic to the Black Lives Matter cause ("I've lived it"), he did not attend any of the protests because he "didn't want to get hurt."

In Retrospect

Often the interviews for this study went way beyond the planned forty minutes. The opening to each interview was to share what they were doing now. Every student talked about themselves, but they also wanted to catch me up on their families too. Then, they wanted to know about me. Many asked about my husband. A few mothers jumped into their children's interview to say hello and share their memories of their child being an Explorer. It seemed that being an Explorer was an experience for the whole family.

Family was a word used to describe the bond we had within the classroom too. For some, being an Explorer was their family. "I had a lot of trouble in my house," explained one student, "and being an Explorer was my get away. I knew everyone cared for me there." Another student expressed, "That classroom was my life! I didn't have a childhood except for that classroom." We all "loved each other," Brandi recalled. She wanted to know if I remembered the day "Travion came into school all sad. We had never seen him that way. He was always happy and had a strong voice. We didn't want him to be sad, so we all just tried to get him to cheer up. He just wanted to be left alone, so we all got sad. We just cared so much about each other."

In her interview, Celina exclaimed, "I just love the Explorers! I am still in touch with so many of them!" Brandi and Celina are still "best friends" and talk all the time. Brandi recently found a class picture and she told me, "I was going through the picture. And I was like, I know everybody's name in here, first and last names. And I was like, oh my gosh, that's how, you know, we were all so close together." "You were like our mom," expressed Farrah. Others, too, described me "like a mom" or a "second mom." Alena elaborated, "I used to love how we were all one little family. That was my main thing right there. We were all so close. And you were really close to all of us." "You cared about what was going on with us," Blakley commented. King closed his interview by telling me, "All classrooms should be like our family of Explorers. I'm glad you are writing a book. Education needs to change."

References

Clark, K. (2016). College prices hit new highs in 2016. *Money*. Retrieved from https://money.com/college-costs-record-2016/.

Gatto, L.A. (2007). Success guaranteed literacy programs: I don't buy it! In J. Larson (Ed.), *Literacy as snake oil* (pp. 73–90). New York, NY: Peter Lang.

Gleeson, P. (2018). The average salary without a degree. *Houston Chronicle*. Retrieved from https://work.chron.com/average-salary-college-degree-1861.html.

Griffith, R. (2008). The impact of a scripted reading program on teachers' professional spirits. *Teaching and Learning*, 22 (3), 121–133.

Hout, M. (2012). Social and economic returns to college education in the United States. *Annual Review of Sociology*, 38 (1), 379–400.

Kneebone, E. & Holmes, N. (2015). The growing distance between people and jobs in metropolitan America. *Metropolitan Policy Program at Brookings*. Retrieved from www.brookings.edu/wp-content/uploads/2016/07/srvy_jobsproximity.pdf.

Kroeger, T., Cooke, T. & Gould, E. (2016). The class of 2016: The labor market still far from ideal for young graduates. *Economic Policy Institute*. Retrieved from www.epi.org/publication/class-of-2016/#epi-toc-4.

Murphy, J. (2018). Rochester's poverty rates worse in new census data. *Democrat & Chronicle*. Retrieved from www.democratandchronicle.com/story/news/2018/12/31/rochesters-poverty-rates-worsen-new-census-data/2449077002/.

NYSED. (2004–2016). *Education statistics reports*. Retrieved from https://data.nysed.gov/archive.php?instid=800000050065.

NYSED. (2015–2016). *High school graduation rates*. Retrieved from https://data.nysed.gov/gradrate.php?year=2016&instid=800000050065.

Owens, C. (2018). Can the city of Kodak and Xerox rebuild its workforce for the digital age? *Next City*. Retrieved from https://nextcity.org/features/view/can-the-city-of-kodak-and-xerox-rebuild-its-workforce-for-the-digital-age.

Torpey, E. (2018). Employment outlook for high school level occupations. *Career Outlook, US Bureau of Labor*. Retrieved from www.bls.gov/careeroutlook/2018/article/pdf/high-school-outlook.pdf.

Yu, M. S., Lombe, M. & Nebbitt, V. E. (2010). Food stamp program participation, informal supports, household food security and child food security: A comparison of African American and caucasian households in poverty. *Children and Youth Services Review*, 32 (5) 767–773.

5 Inclusivity Through Discursive Instruction
Relationships, Social Justice, Belonging

Each students' retrospective interview repeatedly identified themselves as "being an Explorer" in both the past, present, and future tenses. What did that mean to them? From the theoretical coding, three broad dimensions for "being an Explorer" emerged. These three dimensions were: 1) building relationships, 2) engaging in social justice, and 3) feeling a sense of belonging. Discourse analysis was used to interpret and identify these dimensions. The fifteen interview transcripts were analyzed for the frequency of specific words and the regularity in the use of similar words. It was also found that the students consistently indexed their recollections alike and similarly framed their descriptions of building relationships, engaging in social justice, and feeling a sense of belonging.

The fifteen interviews produced over 390 pages of computer-generated transcription and I used these "broad transcripts" for coding (Gee, 2011, p. xi). However, I returned to the video recordings and selected six excerpts from the interviews as exemplars. I transcribed each of these excerpts in detail for further analysis. The six selected transcripts were analyzed using discourse analysis to define and characterize the three dimensions. The transcription excerpts illustrate the students' pauses, word emphasis, and emotion using the following symbols:

! Animated Speech
All Caps Increased Volume
/ Pause
// End of Thought
{ } Action
... Unfinished thought
] [Interruption

DOI: 10.4324/9781003121893-5

Relationships

Every interview referenced relationships as essential to the Explorer community. The data establishes that a multidimensional network of relationships existed within and outside the classroom. These multifaceted relationships included student-teacher relationships, as well as student-student, parent-teacher, community-student, and student-learning relationships. Every student recalled the importance of relationships as part of this dialogic classroom, and these multifaceted relationships permeated every activity.

The interview in the excerpt that follows reveals how Alena reflected upon the relationships within the discursive classroom experience.

Interview Excerpt 1

GATTO: What do you remember about classroom talk as an Explorer?
ALENA: {*claps three times and then laughs*}
I LOVED . . .
Listen/I remember so much from those three years//
They were the most AMAZING years EVER//
I will never forget those . . .
I used to love how we were one little family//
THAT was my main thing right there//
We were all so close//
And YOU were really close to us, especially to me, as a TEACHER//
I didn't only connect with you as a teacher/because of what you did for us //
But I . . .
I HAVE to be hands-on //
And I have to have one on one with my teachers to be able to remember and actually focus //
You did a really great job with that //
And also, me being a BILINGUAL student/you actually had patience with all my wrong words {laughs} when I was speaking and writing //
And the field trips/oh!/the field trips were so AWESOME
{laughs & smiles wide} //
Not only was learning an adventure/but we had so much fun at the same time//
You made school like/just like real life /just put together as one//
I don't know how to explain it //

For Alena, the first word she used to describe her memories of being an Explorer was "love." She raised her voice and used great emphasis for the word "love." She then described the network of relationships within the classroom as "one little family." She again uses emphasis when she said, "THAT," meaning "one little family." She then summarized the love and the feeling of family as her "main thing." Then she reiterated, "We were all so close." Thus, for Alena being an Explorer was membership in a close-knit family where she felt loved.

Then, Alena used the conjunction "and," with the word "YOU." This shifted the topic from the relationship among the class to the relationship she had with me. She begins with, "YOU were really close to us, **especially me**." The comment "especially me" signaled that she felt a special closeness between us. Perhaps she felt even that we had something more special than I had with other students. She began to describe her memory of our personal relationship by telling me, "I didn't only connect with you as a teacher/because of what you did for **us**." Her pause between the two phrases signaled that she connected with me beyond my instructional role. I believe her use of "what you did for us" meant her and her mother. During the first week of school, Alena told me they only brought beds with them from New Jersey, and had no other furniture. I facilitated the donation of furniture to them. There were a few other times when Alena told me they were out of food and I delivered groceries to them. One time, I took Alena grocery shopping after school and drove her home.

Then, Alena used "But I . . ." as a transition and returned to talking about our relationship as student and teacher. She told me, "I HAVE to have hands-on." Her emphasis on "have" reinforced her own self-awareness as a learner. She also explained to me that she needs "one-to-one attention," and that as the teacher, I "did a really good job with that." She also complimented me on my patience with her when she made "mistakes."

It is revealing that the opening question to the interview was, "What do you remember about classroom talk as an Explorer?" and Alena never once directly remembered specific aspects of the classroom talk. Thinking that perhaps she was focusing on the words, "remember" and "Explorer," I rephrased the original question to follow up: "Alena, can you think back to the ways we talked in the classroom?" She then described using the SMARTBoard, working in groups, constructing the longhouse and the museums, and organizing fundraisers. For Alena, remembering the talk in the classroom was integral to the classroom activities and the relationships.

Celina also remembered that our dialogic classroom was in the context of relationships. When asked, "What do you remember about classroom talk as an Explorer?" Celina first described the configuration of the desks in a large square so we all faced one another. The following excerpt is Celina's discussion of the interactions during our classroom talk.

Interview Excerpt 2

CELINA: We were talking like straight to everyone //
So, everyone is looking at your voice/so that everyone was paying attention //
Ummm/because sometimes in a classroom . . .
I've dealt with daycare before /
it's hard to get everyone's attention/especially if they are everywhere/ or they're all faced one way //
I felt like us being in that way //
We were together as a group, like it was more of GROUP TALK //
What is it // {looked away from the screen}
It's/more like it's/like a GROUP CONVERSATION/we would have //
It was something like a team effort //
Instead of like/this kid is answering only and she gets credit //
You know/she gets the sticker/and the other kids /
YOU KNOW/get jealous //
YOU never treated us any different //
You showed all of us LOVE //

Celina explained her memory in relation to the physicality of the desks, "**We** were talking like straight to **everyone**." Her use of "we" and "everyone" indicated she is saying that when one of the Explorers spoke, it was to the whole group. She provided further elaboration when she followed up with, "So **everyone** is looking at **your** voice/so **everyone** is paying attention." Her use of "**your**" in this case implies she is speaking from her personal experience and she is remembering when she spoke in the classroom. Her memory denoted the respectful relationship she had with the other students as a speaker and a listener.

She continued with her memory, but used the discourse marker "umm," which indicated her desire to take a moment to think about what she was going to say next. She then used a personal example beyond the classroom to make a point. She told of her experience as a daycare assistant to make the point that it is hard to get children to listen. Then Celina transitioned back to speaking about the Explorers. She stated, "I felt like us being in **that** way." Her use of "that" referred to her previous statement, "especially if they are **everywhere**/or they're **all faced one way**." In this reference, I believe she is referencing the various ways in which the Explorers conducted talk. It could be in small groups in various locations all over the classroom ("everywhere") or all together at their desks or on the rug ("all faced one way"). This short narrative reinforced her view that the dialogic interactions were based on a respectful relationship among the Explorers.

It seemed important to Celina to correctly name the Explorers' dialogic interactions. First, she labeled the dialogic experience as "together as a group." But then, with a much louder voice, she renamed it "group talk." Immediately, she shifted her gaze away from the screen and asked herself out loud, "What is it?" Finally, she settled on the descriptor "group conversation" in a raised voice. She further clarified when she stated, "It was something like a team effort." She seemed to want to express the importance that our talk included everyone.

She made the comparison to the classrooms she had participated in that conducted talk in an IRE format. IRE is used where the privileging and rewarding of only certain students' correct answers occurs. She describes it as, "This kid is answering only and she gets credit." She deemed this approach as making other students feel excluded ("different") or "jealous." She clearly viewed the dialogic interactions and relationships in the Explorers' classroom as inclusive and fair when she stated, "You never treated us any different, you showed all of us love."

These two excerpts demonstrate just a few of the ways in which students remembered the multidimensional relationships established over the three years. The ways in which the multifaceted relationships were defined and characterized through a discourse analysis of each interview. Table 5.1 illustrates how the multidimensional relationships from the data were defined and characterized.

Social Justice

For this study, social justice is conceptualized as **equal rights and equitable opportunities and treatment for all. In Celina's excerpt earlier she states, "You never treated us any different," which suggests equal treatment within the classroom. She was not the only student to emphasize equal treatment as an Explorer.** In other interviews, it was also articulated that there was access for thinking about and acting upon social justice issues.

Surprisingly, almost every student, without prompting, made comparisons to their other classroom experiences after being an Explorer. These comparisons often spoke about their feelings of injustice in their education and their school district. Finally, the last question in each interview asked the students to share their present activities in political organizations, community memberships, or projects that strive to make change in the world. These findings resulted in social justice being defined in three ways: 1) as a classroom member, 2) as students subsequent to the Explorer experience, and 3) as young adults. Two selected excerpts demonstrate how they were analyzed in the interviews.

Table 5.1 Defining and Characterizing Relationships

Defined As	Characterized As
Teacher-Whole Group Relationships	• Listening to students • Providing opportunities for educational but also personal talk • Valuing all student ideas • Treating students as adults • Sharing personal life • Making learning fun and meaningful • Instituting rituals and routines • Expecting students to work hard and do their best • Caring about students • Maintaining relationships long term on social media and face to face
Teacher-Individual Student Relationships	• Determining the academic needs for each student • Individualizing instruction • Talking personally with each student • Interacting with each students' family • Making them feel special • Interacting with them outside of school
Student-Student Relationships	• Bonding with each other • Looping with each other for three years • Listening to each other • Respecting all ideas • Caring about/loving each other • Negotiating instructional decisions • Accepting/appreciating learning and cultural differences • Maintaining relationships long term on social media and face to face
Parent-Teacher Relationships	• Involving parents in classroom activities • Including parents to accompany overnight field experiences • Having personal interactions with the teacher • Bringing Explorer parents together for events • Arranging events for parents to see their children excel academically • Valuing the non-traditional educational experience of their child being an Explorer • Maintaining long-term connections with other parents and with the teacher • Archiving Explorer artifacts • Reminiscing about Explorer activities
Community-Student Relationships	• Contributing to the community • Being agents of change • Interacting with authority figures • Engaging with professionals in the community

(*Continued*)

Table 5.1 (Continued)

Defined As	Characterized As
Students' Relationship to Learning	• Having fun and adventures • Individualizing experiences • Connecting to real life • Accessing the spaces and materials in the classroom • Talking to learn • Learning from each other

When I asked King if he thought or spoke about the *Lunch is Gross* project since fourth grade, he smiled and related that his capstone project for his Geospatial Technology class made him think about it all the time. He discusses the connection in the following excerpt.

Interview Excerpt 3

KING: My capstone project is on human trafficking //
And I think the research we did for *Lunch is Gross*/made me believe I could change things in the world //
to make things better //
We all saw that we could do that as 4th graders //
It was a real research project/not just look it up on the internet //
After we started conducting surveys and seeing how other schools in the suburbs ate/I NEVER ate school lunches again //
I realized that we deserved better/without telling us/we knew that we were getting bad food because we lived in the city//

In this excerpt, King first expresses what the *Lunch is Gross* project meant to him when he stated, "It made me believe I could change things in the world // to make things better //. Immediately after that, he made the statement, "We all saw that we could do **that** as 4th graders." His use of "that" indexes the object of his previous statement. He meant that all of the Explorers realized their participation in the project made them "believe they could change things in the world" or "make things better."

King then shifted the topic to the surveys we conducted during the project ("after we started conducting surveys"). He was not referring to the student surveys we took within the school, but instead the spreadsheets we constructed to compare menu items between suburban districts and our own ("seeing how other schools in the suburbs ate"). He then reported that as a result of this activity, he "NEVER ate school lunches again." His increased volume for the word "never" implies his emotion and indignation over this issue. It was the only time during his interview that he raised his voice. As a fourth grader, King determined he was going to conduct a boycott of his own and he continued this boycott for the remaining eight years of his schooling in the district.

Finally, in this excerpt, King explained his growing awareness of social inequities. He stated, "I realized that we deserved better," to which he followed up a few sentences later, "We knew that we were getting bad food because we lived in the city." This suggests his feeling of being othered. He does not, however, provide any clues to what he meant by "because we lived in the city." However, later in the interview he articulated the need for change in the significant racial disparities and reminded me that he had "lived experiences as a Black male."

Like King, Shamar had distinct memories of the *Lunch is Gross* project. There were many parallels between their two interviews. The following excerpt of Shamar's interview began with remembering the opening scene of the documentary where Lazarus is holding up the lunch package and wailing as tears drip down his face, "I, I don't like the food and I don't got nothing to eat."

Interview Excerpt 4

SHAMAR: I remember the opening to the movie with Lazarus crying and saying he didn't like the food //
I remember doing the chef project/where we learned to cook three healthy foods/that, that I never ate before //
We did surveys/we surveyed the whole school and made pie graphs with the results //
We even interviewed the lunch ladies //
I remember some didn't want to be interviewed //
We asked one lunch lady/"Why don't you feed this food to your kids?" and she said, "I wouldn't feed it to my dogs." //
I mean/just because the school was serving the lunches/didn't mean I had to eat it //
I realized I could work towards making it better //
Making that movie made me self-advocate //
I learned I had options in life //

As Shamar reminisced about the *Lunch is Gross* project, he focused on the activities where we ate. He remembered cooking healthy foods and foods he "never ate before." Food was particularly significant to Shamar. He was always hungry. He would come to school with bits of cereal or a muffin stored in his pocket, which he would nibble on all morning. Almost daily, he would get caught sneaking food out of the lunchroom. It was because of Shamar that in the middle of second grade, I instituted a snack basket. The snack basket held packets of crackers or small apples. Students could take a snack at any time throughout each day. At first the snack basket was emptied quickly, then after a few days, Shamar was usually the only one who ate from it.

As Shamar turned to a retelling of interviewing the lunch ladies he began with, "We **even** interviewed the lunch ladies." His use of the word "even" indicated that this aspect of the project was unusual to him. For Shamar, most of the adults were always imposing rules and regulations on him. The lunch room monitors in our school were paid staff who were also parents of students in the school. Shamar viewed these staff members as contrary and mean. He was often sent to the principal's office from the lunchroom for getting out of his seat or talking back to the lunch monitors.

He remembered the exact question he asked of the lunchroom monitor of our class table, "Why don't you feed this food to your kids?" Although her son wasn't in our class, he sat at the table next to our class table in the lunchroom. From his question, it seems Shamar knew her children brought their lunches and did not eat school food. His memory of her response ("I wouldn't feed it to my dogs") prompted a reflection, "I mean/just because the school was serving the lunches/didn't mean I had to eat it." His use of the emphasis marker, "I mean," was recognized as his way of expressing disapproval of the school food. Like King, Shamar referred to taking personal action to improve the school food ("I could work towards making it better"). His memory became even more personal when he considered the making of the documentary. "It made me self-advocate," he reflected. He elaborated on self-advocating as "having options in life."

Both of these excerpts exemplify some of the ways in which the issue of social justice impacted the Explorers' actions, expectations, and goals. The interview data demonstrated that these actions, expectations, and goals were substantiated not only as Explorers but also in their subsequent schooling and into their adult lives. These characteristics for social justice were mediated through the dialogic interactions within the Explorer experience. Table 5.2 shows how social justice as an Explorer was defined and characterized from the interview data.

Belonging

The interview data suggested that the idea of belonging was an important concept to every Explorer. In each interview, the students spoke about the

Table 5.2 Defining and Characterizing Social Justice

Defined As	Characterized As
As a Classroom Member	• Taking personal action for change • Taking collective action for change • Challenging authority figures • Standing up/speaking out for injustices • Caring about others different from themselves • Becoming politically active • Being treated equally • Feeling safe to express a viewpoint • Being respected • Speaking up in class
As Students Subsequent to Being an Explorer	• Wanting the right to be heard and make decisions about their education • Wanting to be treated equally • Seeing injustices executed by teachers and the school • Becoming active in school issues • Believing school should be meaningful and exciting • Advocating for themselves
As Young Adults	• Feeling confident • Being aware of and participating in community issues/programs • Advocating for themselves • Challenging authority figures • Voting in local and national elections • Choosing helping or entrepreneurial careers • Wanting to graduate college • Wanting to move out of Rochester • Wanting to escape poverty

Uses the data to create a table depicting all of the ways in which social justice occurred in the dialogic community.

special bonds developed over the three years. As members of a classroom in a large elementary school building, their day was often regulated by bells ringing and imposed schedules for lunch, special subjects, and assemblies. Schoolwide announcements interrupted the classroom activities and lunch was eaten in the crowded all-purpose room with many students from other classes. Yet so many students declared in their interviews, "it just didn't feel like school!" The next two interview excerpts highlight the ways in which the students sensed their feelings of belonging through the constructs of family dynamics, community, and status.

As soon as Luca appeared on screen, he immediately apologized that he might not be able to remember "that much about being an Explorer" because it was so long ago. At first, he spent a lot of time telling me about his present life. Like many of the other interviews, when I asked the first question, "What do you remember about how classroom talk occurred while you were an Explorer?" he did not directly address the question.

Interview Excerpt 5

LUCA: I would say that was probably the best/I probably would say/I was like/the most fortunate child to have grade school in that form //
I feel/like/we were like/the highlight of the whole school/like one of the deals/like/really cool kids //
You would hear about the explorers and like man/
we were the BIG DOGS in the town /
It was great //
GATTO: So/I'm curious to know if you remember anything SPECIFI-CALLY about the way talk occurred in the classroom //
LUCA: But/I mean nothing specifically // how we talked/but I feel like when we talked it was like/our own language //
Between like the words we used or just how we learned //

Luca's answer to my question about classroom talk began with "I was like the most fortunate child to have **grade school in that form**." His use of "in that form" suggests the classroom talk was integral to his experience as an Explorer. He then shifted the topic to explain how he perceived ("I feel like") the way in which the Explorers were viewed by others. He felt that being an Explorer positioned him as part of a community who was "the highlight of the whole school," "one of the deals," and the "really cool kids" of the school. He went on to explain further, "**You** would hear about the Explorers" and "we were the BIG DOGS **in the town**." His use of "you" is a third-person perspective was understood as people in Rochester as he paired it with "in the town." Over the three years, we did have media coverage on the local news, in the school district newsletter, and in the city newspaper.

Just as Luca felt a strong sense of pride and status in being an Explorer, Blakely, too, spoke about her pride in being an Explorer. "I always talk about being an Explorer to my friends," she informed me. Blakely and I were at the end of her interview, but Blakely wasn't ready to end it. She interrupted my close to her interview.

Interview Excerpt 6

GATTO: It was sooo great talking to]
BLAKELY: [I want to thank you //
GATTO: Awww/you don't have to thank me //

BLAKELY: You don't understand/I always talk about being an Explorer to my friends //
I have never had a teacher or professor since you that even cared about me //
You talked to us //
You would know when something was going on in our lives //
And // I'll never forget how you came to my house //
and you took me out for ice cream/when things were really bad one time for me //
School was my get away/my other family.
My own family was so . . . . . . (*her voice lowered and she did not finish the sentence*)

Blakely was not the only student who framed their Explorer experience as family; in fact, more than half the students did. Other students, too, spoke of the classroom as "home." For Blakely, the Explorers were "family" and a "get-away" from her real family. She narrated the time I picked her up at home and took her for ice cream, although I had no recollection of ever doing this. By the middle of second grade, Blakely, along with many other students who lived within walking distance, would beg to stay after school. Long after the dismissal bell rang, students would always stay after to read, create, play games, and write. I would do my work, and they would do theirs. The classroom was a home to many of the Explorers.

Throughout every interview, there was an indication that being an Explorer evoked a strong sense of belonging. The first person plural pronoun "we" was used consistently and constantly throughout every single interview. For example, when Shamar narrated his questioning of the lunch monitor, he said, "**We** asked one lunch lady who was a parent." It was **his** scripted question and **he** posed the question on camera, yet he used **we**, rather than **I**. King spoke for the whole class when he said, "**We** all saw that we could do that as 4th graders." Blakely, too, stated, "I never had a teacher or professor since you that even cared about me." Then, she reiterated the statement with, "You cared about **us**." She used "us" instead of "me." The numerous uses of the first person plural pronoun signals that each student interviewed felt comfortable in representing everyone else in the class.

The sense of belonging was strongly connected to the relationships among the Explorers. As the students remembered being an Explorer, it evoked thoughts of family, caring, and mothering. These impressions were repeated throughout almost every interview. There were a number of interviews where the students disclosed that their siblings or friends were jealous or disappointed that they couldn't be Explorers. Many students shared with me that their families still talk about the activities and events that occurred during those three years.

When Blakely stated, "I have never had a teacher or professor since you that even cared about me," it was striking how many other students compared their other educational experiences and teacher interactions to the ones they had as an Explorer. They seemed to use their Explorer experience as a yardstick to every other classroom experience they have had. Many spoke of the need for a change in education to be "more like what we had" as Explorers. A feeling of belonging in the Explorer classroom included family dynamics, a sense of community, and status.

Inclusivity Through Dialogic Interactions

The three categories of building relationships, engaging in social justice, and feeling a sense of belonging all contributed to the inclusive culture within the Explorer classroom. This inclusive culture was characterized in two different ways throughout the interviews. All of the students interviewed indicated that they felt accepted and respected. They continually stressed how fairly they were treated and how their voices mattered. They felt included.

Table 5.3 Defining and Characterizing Belonging

Defined As	Characterized As
Family Dynamics	• Growing up together • Loving each other • Being "mothered" by the teacher • Having needs met • Feeling safe and nurtured • Sharing their feelings with each other
Community	• Setting goals together • Practices • Working cooperatively • Talking together to learn • Using certain routines • Learning from each other • Sharing responsibilities
Status	• Feeling pride • Having a reputation • Feeling special • Othering by teachers and adults in the school • Being recognized as a member

Uses the data to create a table depicting all of the ways in which a sense of belonging occurred in the dialogic community.

Feeling included and inclusion, however, are not the same thing. Normally, in education, inclusion refers to meeting the educational needs of special education students in the mainstream. However, inclusion does not just pertain to special education students. Inclusion also implies having equal access to opportunities and resources, particularly for students who are excluded or marginalized. By the nature of being urban students, all of these students had already been marginalized by society. Deficit thinking permeated the school and district, which further marginalized many of the students, especially the students who were scoring poorly on standardized tests. The families of the BIPOC students had been systemically marginalized for generations. But as an Explorer, many felt they had been afforded opportunities and resources to insert themselves as equals in their social worlds.

Feeling Included

The most visible indication of feeling included was how every interview used a collective voice throughout many of their memories. Although every question in the interview was asked in the first person, such as, "What do **you** remember about classroom talk?" the transcripts of the students' memories showed the consistent use of plural first person pronouns of "we" and "us" in their answers.

Shamar's use of "we" is the most telling. In his remembering of the making of the video, it was he who interviewed one of the lunch ladies. There were scripted questions, but I remember he went off script using his own knowledge about the lunch lady and her son. It was his own critical question when he asked, "Why don't you feed this food to your kids?" Yet, when he narrated this incident, he retold the memory as if the whole class asked the question ("**We** asked one lunch lady/").

Using the plural first person pronoun instead of "I" and "me" signifies speaking as a collective voice. The consistent and constant use of these plural first-person pronouns throughout every interview represents inclusivity. For example, Alena summed up the three years with, "**We** had so much fun." In Celina's description of classroom talk, she said, "**We** were talking straight to everyone." King considered the impact of the *Lunch is Gross* project from the perspective of the group, not just himself when he stated, "Without telling **us**, **we** knew that **we** were getting bad food because **we** lived in the city."

The excerpts also provide a glimpse into how students felt included through the feelings of acceptance and respect. As a bilingual student, Alena expressed her need for support with learning in English. She remembered the one-to-one learning opportunities as an Explorer which helped her to "remember and actually focus." She also expressed appreciation for the "patience" shown when she used "wrong words when speaking and writing." As a bilingual student, she felt accepted.

Celina described how the interactions were fair when she stated, "You never treated us any different." Celina also expressed how respect and acceptance occurred in the context of classroom conversations. She articulated that all of the students respected one another by speaking to everyone ("we talked straight to everyone") and listening to everyone ("so everyone was paying attention"). Luca described the discursive interactions as having "our own language, between like the words we used, or just how we learned." This suggests that our classroom talk and ways of learning were exclusive and inclusive among the Explorers.

Accessing Equality

As an urban educator, it was important to me that my students had equal access to the same opportunities and resources as their suburban peers. Most of my students had never left their neighborhoods before they became Explorers. A few students expressed their gratitude for the fundraisers, otherwise, they reflected, they would have been unable to accompany the class on the field experiences. But it was clear when Alena exclaimed in her interview, "The field trips, oh! The field trips were so AWESOME!" Her laughter and big smile spoke to her delight in the memories of the many field experiences we shared. She recognized the multiple opportunities the field experiences presented. She also acknowledged the opportunities for learning as "adventure," "fun," and "real life." Shamar, too, indicated his awareness of new opportunities embedded in the learning experiences. He remembered cooking "three healthy meals" and eating "foods I never ate before."

I viewed the architecture of the room as a way of equalizing the resources for my urban students as compared to their suburban peers. I considered the large classroom library, the rich supply of materials and equipment, and the array of classroom pets as a form balancing the rich resources found in suburban elementary classrooms and their personal lives. Over and over, the students remembered the plethora of classroom resources, especially the pets.

Yet, some students remembered the resources in a different way. Some viewed the lessons embedded in meaningful and real-life activities as affording them with valuable resources later in life. King, for example, viewed the "real research" of "conducting surveys" as a resource he used in college for his capstone project. He also regarded the *Lunch is Gross* project as a resource for understanding the concept of social inequality when he asserted, "Without telling us, we knew that we were getting bad food because we lived in the city." Shamar stressed that the experience of participating in the *Lunch is Gross* project as a resource for developing self-awareness and a self-advocating attitude towards his life.

The analysis of these excerpts portrayed the Explorers feeling a strong sense of attachment to this classroom community. The analysis also revealed that the students identified instructional opportunities and resources as inclusive, both academically and as equality. They remembered specific discourse practices that contributed to this culture of inclusion.

Discursive Practices as Inclusive

For three years, the Explorers experienced a discursive pedagogy framed on theories from architecture, situated learning, and power. In my past research, I delved into how this framework mediated voice in the context of classroom interactions. But, in this retrospective study, the framework was used to understand the student memories of that classroom talk. The discursive practices that emerged from the student interviews as creating feelings of being included and of inclusion were located within the framework (Figure 5.1).

The discursive practices highlighted in the students' memories were shaped by and shaped the classroom environment, the community culture, and the power dynamics of the classroom. These practices visibly aligned to the framework for an inquiry-based instruction to create an "interactional inclusion" (Rex, 2001). Rex suggests that inclusive classrooms "require a re-visioning of what is meant by curriculum, instruction, and assessment" (p. 122). Rex advocates for a re-visioning that includes centralizing discourse in meaningful and interconnected contexts, where students are producers of knowledge instead of consumers. The interviews of the Explorers evoked memories of a classroom where a re-visioning of curriculum, instruction, and assessment had occurred. The re-visioning for dialogic pedagogy in this classroom was constituted by the shifting participation frameworks, negotiating authority, and developing group identity.

Shifting Participation Frameworks

In classrooms where IRE dominates the rules and the roles or participation frameworks, for students' and teachers' participation were quite clear and familiar. Contrasting this known discourse pattern was the use of a dialogic

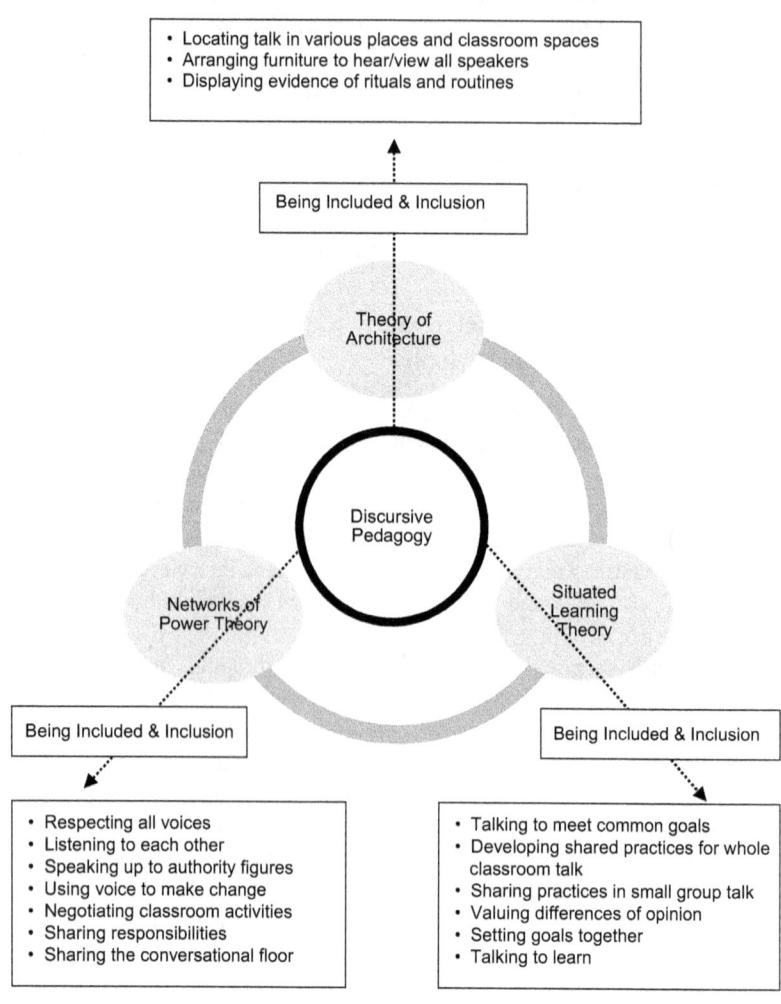

Figure 5.1 Inclusive Practices for Discursive Pedagogy

participation framework. In the interviews, the students clearly recognized that the classroom talk as an Explorer was atypical to the familiar talk that occurred in their other educational experiences. However, they had difficulty putting a name to it, or even describing it. Celina's excerpt was like many of the others. She used three descriptors ("were together as a group," "group talk," and "group conversation"). Until she finally settled on the term "a team effort." This was representative of the difficulty some of the students had in describing the participation frameworks of the discursive practices in the Explorer classroom. One student stated, "I've never been in a classroom except, with the Explorers, where we didn't raise our hands to speak."

Our participation framework for discursive practices also included daily rituals and routines. Every day we would begin a transition to another subject using a chant. For example, each morning our first subject was reading. We would gather together on the rug and begin by chanting and clapping, "Reading Club! Reading Club! YAY! YAY! YAY! Reading Club! Reading Club! Let's have some fun today!" We had a chant for Math Minds and Writers Workshop, too. The impetus for these chants began a few weeks into second grade. I called the students to the rug to begin Reading Club, and as a student was walking to the rug, she began to chant in a sing song voice, "Reading Club, YAY, YAY, YAY," and then repeated it. I impulsively added, "Let's have some fun today! Hey!" A few students put the two chants together and I wrote it down on the chart paper. From that day on, it was the chant we used as the start of reading club every day. Someone suggested we needed to have a chant for Math Minds and Writers Workshop. So, we co-constructed chants for the start of those two daily instructional periods, too. This is just one example of how this dialogic classroom became re-visioned through meaningful and negotiated discourse where students were producers of knowledge instead of consumers.

In another example, a few students remembered that there were times my role was as a note taker of their words. They remembered that their ideas were incorporated into lessons and projects. "We told you what to write to the principal and you wrote it," remembered one student, as he recalled the letter we co-constructed asking for a few Explorers to visit a suburban lunchroom. He was describing my position in the center of the desks, sitting on a stool scribing on my computer as the SMARTBoard screen projected what I wrote.

The students also remembered that they "had a voice" as they recalled their memories of classroom talk. Many also remembered the classroom as a space where they could contribute their ideas for lessons. One student explained that, to her, the classroom talk seemed like a "collaboration, we discussed things back and forth. We talked while we worked, about the work!" Another student remembered that through the classroom talk, "we shared our knowledge with each other." In their memories, this classroom offered a dialogic space that sparked creativity, new knowledge, and co-constructed texts. This was another example of students who remembered the classroom talk positioning them as not just consumers of knowledge, but also producers of knowledge.

It is an important consideration that this class looped together for three years. Abigail reflected in her interview, "Looping provided no buffer from one year to the next, we would just pick up where we left off." As a community of learners, their enrollment remained static for the entire three years. Every student entered the Explorers as second graders having had traditional school experiences as kindergarteners and first graders. Five of the students had repeated a grade already. They were all beginners to the dialogic practices of this re-envisioned classroom. Over that span of time, embedded repertoires of practice had become deeply familiar, particularly for classroom talk.

It took months of role playing, videotaping, and modeling for the students to understand how to have whole class discussions without raising their hands. They were so unaccustomed to speaking to anyone but the teacher. At first, they resisted speaking to each other and actually listening to each other. Slowly, their participation shifted from being passive learners to being learners who actively spoke and listened. During the end of our last year together, I noted in my journal:

> Today the room buzzed with activity as the groups worked on their model homes. I sat at the back table waiting for requests for help and/or filling their requests for materials purchases. But no one came. No one called my name, no one asked for help, no one even spoke to me (for at least for ten minutes!). Everyone worked confidently and continually within their small groups. They talked across groups to share what they were doing. One group was having trouble with their wiring and asked another group to help them figure out the problem. I think my job is done here!

After three years as Explorers, the students had adopted a fluidly shifting dialogic participation framework; they entered as "newcomers," but had become "old timers" (Lave & Wenger, 1991). These old timers had developed a new set of participation frameworks. In his interview, Shamar listed them:

- We didn't raise our hands;
- We didn't talk over each other. We just waited for our turn;
- Everybody was involved;
- If you didn't agree with someone, it was expected you would respect their opinion; and
- Everybody had something to learn from someone else.

Teaching and learning for the Explorers had become a dialogic pedagogy. The shift from the known IRE participation framework to a dialogic one was documented in my case study of these students. Thirteen years later, the student interviews validated this conclusion. This shift in our participation frameworks also shifted the network of power within the classroom culture.

Negotiating Authority

I recognize authority as a social construct determined by complex interactions (Metz, 1978). A significant finding of my earlier research determined that authority became a negotiated accomplishment during whole class talk. In this case study, authority was conceptualized through the whole group talk. In this context, authority became an interactional accomplishment consisting of 1) *in* control, 2) *to* control, and 3) *for* control. Authority *in* control described the jointly held processes and structures that managed classroom actions, classroom rules, and the conversational floor. The students and teacher positioned their authority *to* control what counts as knowledge, who is knowledgeable, and how instruction is organized. Authority *for* control can be characterized as the teacher and students reacting together to outside forces such as rules, inequity, and discrimination.

It was my goal to have students actively produce knowledge, recognize what constrained them from success, and broaden their social worlds. To achieve these goals, I would have to push back on the institutional authority that surrounded me, while at the same time relinquish some of my own authority in the classroom. It was clear to anyone who observed in or participated with the Explorers that I was the authority figure and *in* control. I could be demanding and commanding. I had high expectations for my students. Two students recalled, "We worked hard." However, I tried to use my authority "reflexively" and provide spaces for "students to exercise intellectual rigor, theoretical competence, and informed judgements" (Giroux, 2001, p. 105).

The discursive instruction provided many opportunities for negotiating authority among the Explorers. When students returned from lunch and complained about the school food, they were *in* control. As they planned and built a shared vision of the documentary, they were not only *in* control, but also it was *to* control.

Students were *in* control when their comments or questions altered the direction of the lesson or discussion. But when the students took control of the topic and built a shared vision, it was *to* control.

There were many other times when students led the conversation or held the floor for long periods. The Spotlight on the Author was one such practice where students not only held the floor for long periods of time, but also controlled the conversational floor. A gooseneck lamp was clamped to the top shelf of a tall bookcase. Underneath it sat a tall stool. The students would sign up to take turns reading their authored texts. We would turn on the spotlight and all attention was on the author. I would introduce a student to read aloud about three minutes of their text, then I would select three students to offer compliments and suggestions, or ask questions. It was the only time Explorers raised their hands to speak. I explained it was to ensure that the author didn't just call on their friends. Over the course of our first year together, students promised they wouldn't just call on their friends. At some point, the turn taking was relinquished to the student author, and even I had to raise my hand to be selected to speak. The student under the spotlight not only controlled who spoke, but could also ask for clarification from the commenter.

The students had negotiated authority *for* control of Spotlight on the Author. As a result, they had become *in* control of this discursive practice. They had also negotiated the authority *to* control whose knowledge counted for feedback on their writing.

Perhaps, Abigail's remark of "I never had another teacher like you, not even in college. The teachers always led the discussion" was remembering the numerous times she controlled the conversational floor as she read her writing and determined who gave her feedback under the spotlight. Shamar certainly recalled this discursive instruction as a time "where everybody engaged on the author. Whoever was under the spotlight got all the attention." He remembered the discursive interactions as being *to* control and *in* control.

Although there were only a few interview quotes that suggested authority being negotiated *to* control and *in* control, there were many statements that articulated how our dialogic interactions were *for* control. The most obvious example were their memories of producing the *Lunch is Gross* documentary. This interactional accomplishment was remembered as *for* control in reaction to the school district's food service provider. The process of producing the video was also remembered as using classroom talk *for* control. Seth described the time we wrote to a suburban principal requesting a visit to their school lunchroom. "We wrote to a principal and she didn't respond, so we decided to send it up to the next person. I think it was the superintendent." He remembered the interactional accomplishment of authority *for* control.

Farrah, too, described authority as an interactional accomplishment *for* controlling. She reminisced about eating lunch with the superintendent and being able to actually show him how bad the food was. She remembered spending time as a class writing the speech she would give at the school board meeting. And she viewed picketing in front of the district's central office as "fighting for our rights."

Shor (1996) wrote, "We don't come to class with the discourse habits suitable for reconstituting power relations. We have to invent that discourse as we invent the process, and by doing so, reconstruct our social selves" (p. 20). In the case of the Explorers, our discursive practices contributed to reconstituting the role of authority within our interactions and, ultimately, influenced the establishing a group identity.

Developing Group Identity

According to Wenger (1998), identity in relation to a community of practice "is a way of talking about how learning changes who we are and creates personal histories of becoming in the context of our communities" (p. 5). Some of the students identified the ways in which being an Explorer influenced their personal histories of "becoming" in the context of their experience of being an Explorer. Zahara acknowledged that she writes every day since her mom died, just like we used to write in the "Between You and Me" journals. Blakely stated, "I'm in college and that has everything to do with being an Explorer. If I hadn't been an Explorer, I would have never stayed in school. It made me love school and learning." In her interview, Farrah articulated her desire to "seriously travel the world, just like we did as Explorers." King expressed that being an Explorer "made me believe in myself." Brandi credits the dialogic practices of the classroom to contributing to her identity. She reflected how shy she was and then remembered, "I ended up talking a lot and just being me. I just made my voice be heard. I would have never found it in any other classroom, if I didn't have that voice." But "Being an Explorer" not only contributed to individual identities, but also group identity.

In every student interview there was a characterization of a group identity. My initial reasoning for naming my classes was in response to the way I had heard teachers address their class when getting their attention. Many of my colleagues used "boys and girls," "children," or even "you guys." None of those felt right to me. Using a class name to address my students seemed like a great solution. Whenever I spoke to or about the class, I used the name they had chosen for themselves, "The Explorers." The students, too, spoke of their participation in this classroom as being an Explorer. "Being an Explorer" denoted a group identity. It was heard over and over again in the interviews. "I will always be an Explorer," said four of the students. Thirteen years after being an Explorer, they still felt bonded to the group membership. "We grew up together," explained one student.

The group identity of "Being an Explorer" seemed to have diverse meanings. As if he was speaking for all of the Explorers, Shamar told me, "Being an Explorer made us all want to be good students." Brandi described an emotional connection to being an Explorer. She stated, "there was always joy, we never wanted anyone to be sad." But she also connected the group identity to learning. She explained, "We learned new things together as a whole." Then she continued, "We built upon that (learning new things). We would work together and built that bond. We made the best classroom that I can think of, better than any other kids."

Brandi's comment about being a better class than any of the other kids was echoed from other students. As Keagan discussed going into fifth grade after spending three years as an Explorer, he explained that the kids in his fifth grade class who were not Explorers asked, "Hey, you were in that really cool class? What happened in that class?" Then, Seth declared that "everyone in the school wanted to be in our class." Luca concurred, "We were a group of kids that everyone else wanted to be." Their group identity was elevated to a prestigious status among the other students in the school.

Creating opportunities for students to participate in meaningful practices gave students a meaningful identity (Wenger, 1998). The Explorer classroom was never "just an accumulation of skills and information, but a process of becoming" (Wenger, 1998, p. 215). It was a community of practice where the production of knowledge brought "the community together to give it its identity" (Wenger & Wenger-Trayner, 2015, para. 13).

Re-Imagining Discursive Instruction

The students often expressed that they viewed being an Explorer as being an "insider" where they viewed their classroom experience as somehow different from others. They believed the Explorers had their own way of "thinking, acting, interacting, valuing, and believing" (Gee, 2003, p. 27). This retrospective study explored the nature and impact of a re-imagined discursive approach to teaching and learning. The classroom talk they described was a responsive/collaborative script where the participation frameworks were atypical, authority was negotiated, and a strong group identity developed. The students described this interactional dialogic space as a unique and exceptional educational experience. After thirteen years, the memories and reflections from the fifteen students who were Explorers noted the experience as being highly valued. Many expressed it as life changing. The shifting of participation frameworks, negotiating of authority, and developing a group identity over time constituted a powerful approach to re-imaging dialogic pedagogy.

References

Gee, J.P. (2003). *What video games have to teach us about learning and literacy.* New York, NY: Palgrave.

Gee, J.P. (2011). Discourse Analysis: What Makes it Critical? In Rogers, R. (Ed.), *An introduction to critical discourse analysis in education.* New York, NY: Routledge.

Giroux, H.A. (2001). *Public space, private lives: Beyond the culture of cynicism.* New York, NY: Rowman & Littlefield Publishers.

Lave, J. & Wenger, E. (1991). *Situated learning: Legitimate peripheral participation*. New York, NY: Cambridge Press.

Metz, M.H. (1978). *Classrooms and corridors: The crisis of authority in desegregated secondary schools*. Berkeley, CA: University of California Press.

Rex, L.A. (2001). The remaking of a high school reader. *Reading Research Quarterly*, 36 (3), 288–314. Retrieved from www.academia.edu/573315/Judy_constructs_a_genuine_question_A_case_for_interactional_inclusion.

Shor, I. (1996). *When students have power: Negotiating authority in a critical pedagogy*. Chicago, IL: The University of Chicago Press.

Wenger, E. (1998). *Communities of practice: Learning, meaning and identity*. New York, NY: Cambridge University Press.

Wenger-Trayner, E. & Wenger-Trayner, B. (2015). *Introduction to communities of practice: A brief overview of the concept and its uses*. Retrieved from https://wenger-trayner.com/introduction-to-communities-of-practice/.

6 Living Dialogue and Authority in the Elementary Classroom
Insights to Inform Practice

In 1988, Sutter and Grensjö reported on their research and development project promoting an authentic research project with students. They viewed this project as going beyond what children learn from books. Explorative learning was "an attempt to break out of the vicious circle of only reproductive activity" (p. 47). The classroom research conversations occurred within and beyond the classrooms and so they identified these conversations and classroom interactions as part of a "living dialogue."

Theorists and philosophers have also referred to language interactions as living dialogue.

Bahktin (1981) regards a living dialogue as "directly, blatantly, oriented toward a future answer, where there is an "atmosphere of the already spoken" (p. 280). For Bahktin, a living dialogue anticipates an answer. Buber provides a more in-depth concept of a living dialogue. Buber in his book, *I and Thou: Practicing Living Dialogue* (2003), describes a living dialogue as an intersubjective relationship. Within this dialogic intersubjective relationship, an orientation of turning towards the other creates a space for understanding the other's perspective. Buber's four principles for a living dialogue are turning toward, addressing affirmatively, listening attentively, and responding responsibly to engage.

Wegerif (2013), too, views a living dialogue as an intersubjective relationship. He characterizes it as an "openness towards the other" (p. 142). Consequently, a living dialogue is "unpredictable and unbounded in its potential because nobody can get outside of it and tell you where it will go and what its limits are" (p. 6). In a recent blog post on dialogic research, Wegerif (2019) describes a living dialogue as the tension between the emic and etic perspectives where "the subjects of the research moving from the inside out and the view that is trying to define and locate that experience moving from the outside in" (para 6).

The phrase "living dialogue," then, suggests the occurrence of a thoughtful conversation between two or more conversants. A living dialogue implies

DOI: 10.4324/9781003121893-6

the conversants are considering the perspective of the others in the conversation, while also representing their own perspective. But the phrase "living dialogue" seems to hint at so much more, especially when it is used to describe dialogic pedagogy in the elementary classroom.

Living Dialogue in the Classroom

Sutter and Grensjö viewed their research project as a social endeavor. Their approach to "explorative learning" was to engage various grade levels in conducting research using local historical and town hall records. As they authentically conducted research, students and teachers engaged with community members. This process required a network of relationships beyond the classroom. It was also meant to generate subjective knowledge to be shared with the public.

From their research, they identified explorative learning as having four conditions: 1) students and teacher together conduct empirically based research, 2) establishing new relations between and among students and teachers, 3) new conditions of learning emerge, and 4) teachers and students learn together (p. 42). These conditions focus on the process of learning, not the acquisition of facts. Sutter and Grensjö described the resulting classroom talk as a living dialogue. They explain that a living dialogue "implies running the risk of not doing well, of losing the shelter of formal authority, but it also means the possibility of acquiring new authority based on professional competence." They warned it could have a "demoralizing effect of power on instruction" (p. 48).

Willbergh and Aasebø (2018) conducted an empirical analysis of lesson structures in Norwegian high schools in the Netherlands. They found typical to most lesson structures was a plenary conversation. They describe plenary conversations as "teacher led, but organized as a conversation in which the students participated" (p. 5). This conversation was often structured as a recitation script, but also shifted to a responsive script when teachers used open-ended questions. In response, students incorporated their own experiences, interpretations, and opinions. Within this student contribution, they used their "mother tongue creating the class' local interpretation of subject matter" (Willbergh, 2016). When the plenary conversations shifted to a responsive script, Willbergh and Aasebø described it as a living dialogue.

Both of these studies mention living dialogue in the context of observing classroom interactions, yet there is no clear interpretation of what a living dialogue actually is. Thinking about the dialogic interactions as I have researched them, the ways in which my students remembered them, and the few mentions in the literature, I have concluded that the dialogic interactions between and among the Explorers was a living dialogue. The in-depth analysis of my students' memories reimagines the ways in which classroom talk can be a living dialogue.

Theoretical Foundations for Dialogic Teaching

The significant studies of dialogic classrooms by Nystrand, Mercer, and Michaels and O'Conner discussed in Chapter 1 have identified the pragmatics for conducting effective classroom conversations. Alexander (2020) expands upon this research to offer a framework for a foundational stance for dialogic teaching. He first introduces six principles which establish the "criteria" for the kinds of talk that can occur in a dialogic classroom (p. 131). He argues that teachers can use these principles for guiding and managing a dialogic classroom. The students in this view are empowered to become "speakers, thinkers, reasoners, learners, and evaluators" (p. 119). The Explorers remembered experiencing the six principles that Anderson described. Table 6.1 illustrates how Alexander's six principles were articulated by the Explorers' memories.

Table 6.1 Explorer Memories of Anderson's Six Principles

Anderson's Principles for Dialogic Teaching	Explorer Memories
Joint Learning (Learning tasks together)	• "We always worked in teams. • "Everything was done working with others." • "I remember working in small groups on so many projects." • "We made so many decisions and thought about so much together."
Supportive (Expressing ideas freely with no risk for embarrassment or judgement)	• "My English was not that good, but I was never afraid to talk in front of the group." • "You got us quiet kids to talk." • "We weren't judged by the others."
Reciprocal (Listening to each other; sharing ideas; asking questions; providing alternate viewpoints)	• "We heard everyone's point of view." • "We talked straight to everyone." • "Everyone paid attention to whoever was talking." • "Everybody was involved. If you didn't agree with someone, it was expected that you would respect their opinion."
Deliberative (Discussing, presenting, resolving, and evaluating differences)	• "We communicated with each other. We had to base our answers on facts or evidence and then others would answer back. They had to use facts too." • "We discussed things back and forth."

(*Continued*)

Table 6.1 (Continued)

Anderson's Principles for Dialogic Teaching	Explorer Memories
Cumulative (Building upon one another's statements; listening and responding for understanding)	• "We learned new things as a whole group, and then we built upon that to learn other new things." • "Everybody had something to learn from someone else."
Purposeful (Structuring for specific learning goals)	• "We wanted to see our hard work actually do something." • "Our work and talk was always productive." • "We knew how to talk with respect to each other." • "We talked to learn."

Uses the data to create a table depicting all of the ways in which relationships occurred in the dialogic community.

At the core of Alexander's framework for dialogic teaching is a compilation of repertoires for dialogic practices. These eight repertoires were incorporated into the daily life of the Explorers (Alexander's repertoires have been italicized). The *interactive culture* included a shared understanding of the ways in which talk was managed within the differing participation frameworks of whole group, small groups, partners, and one-to-one with the teacher. As highlighted in previous chapters, the Explorers were taught expectations for talk. They knew that the teacher would not be calling on them and they were to self-select. They learned to wait for an opening and not to interrupt the speaker. There were daily rituals that included chants to initiate transitions, and they knew the structure of each lesson. For example, the structure of Reading Club (our name for the reading instructional block) always began on the rug with a read aloud. I introduced the objective for the read aloud lesson posted on the easel. This introduction might be a question or an incomplete chart posted on large chart paper. Our dialogic interactions focused on the objective of the lesson, and throughout the lesson, I scribed the ideas and notes the students talked about on the chart paper. The lesson would end with a summation made by myself. An independent project would be used as a follow-up to the read aloud lesson. While the students worked either alone or in small groups (self-selected), I would call three different flexible reading groups to work on specific reading objectives for about twenty minutes each. I also spent about ten minutes after meeting with these groups to work with a small remedial group every day. If students finished their independent project, they would self-select a center activity, or buddy reading or silent reading. Reading Club ended with a few students sharing their independent project with the class, summarizing the lesson objective. Throughout each of these participation frameworks, the roles and talk in action varied. The Explorers' memories validated the shared understanding of the ways in which talk was managed in the *interactive culture* of their looped classroom.

The *interactive setting* positioned interactions as inclusive and independent. The classroom environment was vividly remembered by every student. They clearly connected the physical environment to the various dialogic interactions they had during classroom activities. The organization of dialogic groups varied from activity to activity. The formation of these groups was often determined by the teacher, but students were also given opportunities to self-select the membership of their working groups. Students understood the dialogic expectations for working in groups, and could independently talk for successfully completing a project.

The Explorers *learned to talk* using particular forms of talk by considering register, vocabulary, and audience. Their memories were very clear on being respectful dialogic speakers and listeners. In their interviews, they remembered their participation in numerous field experiences and exhibitions, which allowed them multiple opportunities for shifting their registers and using formal patterns of talk. These experiences, along with the classroom talk, supported them in asking questions, explaining their ideas, sharing information, and making arguments.

As the teacher, my *teaching talk* was intentional and the shifting of discourse scripts were continual. We could fluidly move from a recitation script to collaborative/dialogic script and then back to a recitative script within a matter of a few minutes. All three scripts overlapped one another and intersected. I had become skilled at using classroom talk to prompt student talk. I planned the thematic units but I knew their ideas, questions, and connections would make them come alive and be meaningful. The students knew I valued their dialogic interactions.

My *questioning* used multiple forms of talk moves. As small groups worked on science or math investigations, I would enter their discussions by asking, "So what is going on here?" This open-ended question allowed me to understand how the students were approaching their task and what they were understanding or misunderstanding. I also used questions to manage procedures, clarify statements, probe and expand thinking, and elaborate ideas. Productive questions (Martens, 1999) were also part of my tool box for questioning. Productive questions "enable a teacher to provide scaffolding for students beginning to build their own understandings" (p. 24).

Extending the dialogue was also an intentional talk move and closely connected to the questioning. But it could also be a spontaneous moment where I would pick up on something the students would question or say.

Such as, that day after lunch when in exasperation I asked, "So, what are you going to do about it?" That question prompted a lengthy discussion that led to a project rich in literacy and math learning.

Finally, *discussing and arguing* were achieved through dialogic exchanges during all subjects. The skills for making a good argument were taught intentionally. I introduced making an argument using science investigations. The Explorers used their evidence to make claims. When students had different results, they would discuss to examine the procedures and possible reasons for the discrepancy. This form of discourse spilled into the other subjects. The chart paper that I would scribe on during read aloud was often used for making an argument. A student would flip through the compilation of chart paper to refer back to previous notes as evidence.

Alexander's principles and repertoires were all evidenced in my classroom discourse. In fact, the Explorers' classroom experience embodied Alexander's framework for dialogic teaching. Yet, the research on dialogic classrooms did not have to demonstrate or indicate the same outcomes as this retrospective study. The students' memories evoked loyalty, enthusiasm, and a passion for the dynamics that occurred in their Explorer classroom. I argue that this dialogic classroom was a re-envisioned classroom in the form of a living dialogue.

Authority and a Living Dialogue

Sutter and Grensjö's described living dialogue as "losing the shelter of formal authority but it also means acquiring a new authority based on professional competence" (p. 48). In a recent interview (Asterhan, Howe, Lefstein, Matusov & Reznitskaya, 2020), Matusov spoke of authority in relation to dialogic pedagogy:

> I like Bakhtin's notion of "consciousnesses with equal rights," when, again, basically, it's about the collapse of authority. First of all, it's about the collapse of institutional authority and teacher authority. I like the idea that dialogue cannot be forced. It's always voluntary. So school, conventional school, is anti-dialogical in this sense because it's often mandatory – society wants education for all students and defines what this education is about. And I like dialogue, in which the primary focus is not on the agreement and the consensus but on the misunderstanding, non-understanding, disagreements, puzzlement, and so forth.

For the Explorers, authority became an interactional accomplishment where authority was jointly negotiated and socially constructed within the dialogic interactions of the classroom.. Being *in* control, positioning *for* control, or attempting *to* control were weaved throughout the whole class talk by both teacher and students. Within the living dialogue, classroom talk usually followed the norms established for "talking the way adults do," but these participation frameworks could be fractured by the insertion of:

- spontaneous outbursts,
- overlapping speech,
- personal topics,
- interruptions,
- side conversations,
- movement,
- off-topic conversations,
- loud and/or lively voices, and
- emotions.

As an Explorer, authority as an interactional accomplishment did not apply to just the conversational floor of the classroom. One of our biggest fundraisers was a candy bar sale. Two students had the idea to sit outside the lunchroom a few minutes before lunch began so they could sell candy bars. Off they went with a box of candy bars and a large sign they had made to advertise the sale. When I brought the rest of the class to the lunchroom, the principal approached me and announced that the students could not sell candy at lunch time. I took the box, the sign, and the money they had collected from their sales back upstairs with me. When I returned to the lunchroom, the students circled around me to tell me they were going to sell the candy bars to the parents who arrived early to pick their children up at the end of the day. On this day, authority became an interactional accomplishment *to* control the power dynamics between themselves and the principal. The Explorers came to view power as productive "rather than repressive and negative" (Popkewitz, 1999, p. 5).

In their interviews, some of the Explorers expressed how they are still using authority *to* control the power dynamics in their present day lives. As a Black student attending a predominantly white college, Blakely talked about her experience with that, she told me. "Somebody said something on social media and I just kind of had enough," she explained. "So, I took action and made my voice heard. We picketed and spoke with the dean. I knew if they didn't make a change, there would be nothing for me on that campus. But we did make change." Abigail, too, had an experience at her college where some of the students pushed back on the power dynamics. She and a group of students met with the vice president of the school. "He just talked right over us, so we left, and then we picketed in front of the main hall. Then, he listened to us."

In my previous research, it was determined that the outcome of authority as an interactional accomplishment was critical literacy. This meant that the Explorers not only considered the power networks they engaged with, but also the texts and language of the "regimes of truth."

To assist Seth in creating the multiple choice clicker game for the dinosaur museum, I explained and demonstrated for the class the thinking behind how these tests are constructed. A few months later, the Explorers took the state reading standardized test, which was a multiple choice test. When the test results were returned to me, I noticed that Shamar's score had met the standards. I was shocked, knowing that his reading ability was far below the standards. When I asked him how in the world he did so well on the test, he smiled and told me remembered what I had shown about how the test makers think. Shamar had pushed back on the "regime of truth."

As in the case of the *Lunch is Gross* project, students also used critical literacy and authority as an interactional accomplishment to acknowledge local realities. They designed and redesigned texts for real-world purposes. These texts often had a political or social intent. In each of their museums, there were clear messages for social or ecological responsibilities. In the Haudenosaunee Museum, some of the students created posters about being kind to Mother Nature and caring about the earth. Two students created a display of how every part of the deer was used after killing it. They wanted the museum visitors to know not to waste anything. These points of view were developed from meeting members of the Haudenosaunee tribe and reading about their culture.

The forms of authority that circulated through our dialogic interactions established the students as active subjects. The lines of the traditional classroom relationships were blurred. King told me in his interview, "Anyone who walked into that classroom knew you cared about the students and if they learned, and that the students cared about each other and about learning." It was bell hooks (1989) who described "moving from silence to speech . . . that makes new life and new growth possible. It is the movement from object to subject – the liberated voice" (p. 9). The Explorers identified themselves as a group of elementary school students who had been liberated.

Conceptualizing a Living Dialogue

Clearly, the term "living dialogue" has been under conceptualized. Using the analysis from this retrospective study, the concept of a living dialogue becomes more thoroughly visualized. The students who experienced the inquiry-based pedagogy, as described in Chapter 2, clearly recalled interacting in the classroom environment, interacting with power networks, and working towards common goals. All of these interactions shaped and were being shaped by discursive pedagogy. In Chapter 5, the discourse analysis of the interview transcripts demonstrated how the dialogic interactions in the classroom generated a culture of inclusion through the shifting participation frameworks, the negotiating of authority, and building a strong group identity.

In Chapter 2, I introduced a figure (Figure 2.1) depicting the framework for the way in which I frame an inquiry-based pedagogy. I built upon that figure in Chapter 5 to demonstrate how the discursive pedagogy mediated by the theories created inclusive practices (Figure 5.1). Then I layered critical literacy and the three analytical categories that conceptualizes how the dialogic pedagogy engaged the Explorers in a living dialogue (Figure 6.1).

A living dialogue embodies the research-based practices of multiple approaches to teaching "through, for, and as dialogue" (Kim & Wilkinson, 2019, p. 70). For the Explorers, it meant going beyond academic achievement. Their culture, interests, and histories were legitimized. They remembered the living dialogue as:

- talking together,
- respecting everyone's words and right to speak,
- prompting their creativity,
- increasing their motivation,
- generating and sharing new knowledge,
- setting goals,
- caring about each other, and
- acting upon injustice.

It was within the face-to-face interactions of authentic and meaningful classroom activity where a living dialogue emerged. Student voice, choice, and agency developed. The classroom became a place where student authority was valued. A living dialogue was also a space for students to develop caring relationships, be inclusive, and to act for improving their own world. In a living dialogue, the teacher shapes the curriculum and the classroom interactions, but it is the students, through their talk, who enact it. A living dialogue is a co-constructed, interactional achievement.

Living Dialogue for Informing Practice

The global neo-liberal agenda has shifted education policy and practices. The competing voices of economics, politics, and ideologies have halted the momentum of creative and innovative approaches for teaching. Teachers

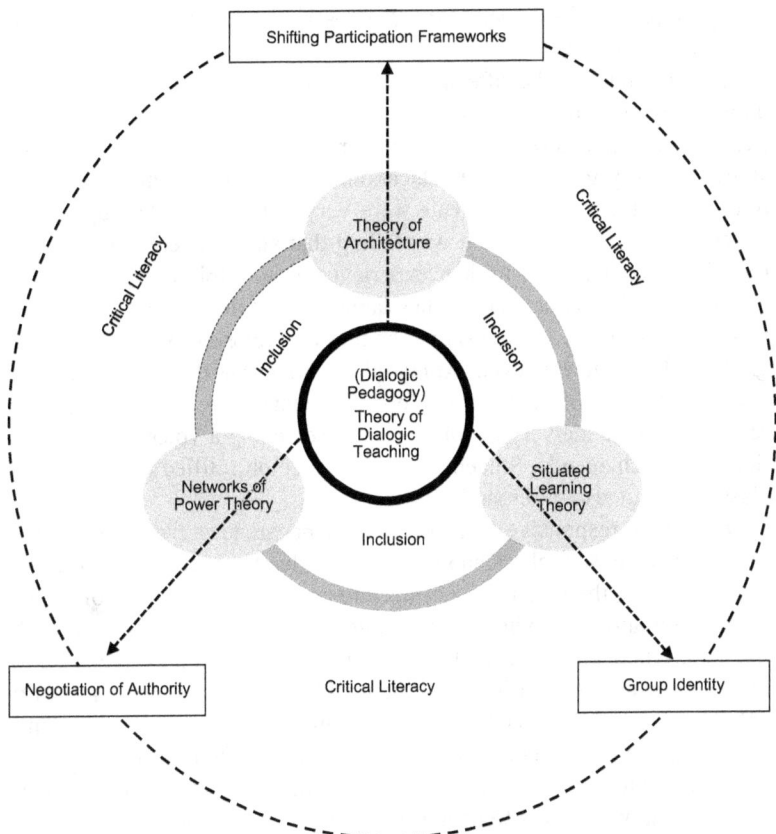

Figure 6.1 Conceptualizing a Living Dialogue

have been deskilled and the curriculum has become commodified. Classrooms have become "identified with an economic value system that shapes all reality in its own image" (Brancaleone & O'Brien, 2011, p. 502). Thus, educational research has been shaped by the neoliberal agenda too.

There is a vast amount of research on dialogic classrooms that offers conclusive evidence for its effectiveness, yet so little has changed at the classroom level. The highly structured, teacher-controlled classroom discourse governs most classrooms around the word. Educational researchers need to provide further documentation and analysis of classrooms where living dialogues occur. I urge researchers to find classrooms where living dialogues are taking place and to spend time in them to understand how the teacher's instructional theories, the classroom discourse, and the outcomes connect. There are classrooms across the country where living dialogues are taking place. The field needs far more descriptive and theorized accounts of those classrooms.

The interviews of the fifteen Explorers provided a rich data corpus for understanding the dialogic interactions in their second to fourth grade experience. I recommend researchers consider the use of the retrospective case study as a way to understand educational experiences from the perspective of the students. My students were very willing to reflect upon their experiences as an Explorer. It was telling that almost every student made unsolicited comparisons to their experience as an Explorer to their subsequent educational experiences. They lamented that the Explorer experience was unique and that "school should be that way for everyone and for every grade." Three students even expressed the hope that the book will affect change in the school experience before their own children go to school. Few researchers give the very people we are researching a voice in the educational research agenda. Students continue to be objectified not only in the classroom, but also in research.

Dialogic or responsive/collaborative scripts are least likely to be found in high-poverty schools (Knapp, 1995). I understand all too well the limited resources, the inferior materials and equipment, and most of all, the controlling and constraining curriculum that permeates the urban teaching experience. I never let that stand in my way or used it as an excuse for not doing what was best for my students. I believed teaching was a political act; I wanted the very best possible education for my urban students, believing that a good education could be a way to fight back at the cycle of poverty and the systemic racism that permeated many of my students' lives. My approach was to be a professional and intellectual teacher.

One approach I used was to articulate my instructional methods to my administrators. I submitted thematic unit plans that articulated my theoretical reasoning and instructional thinking. Each unit plan included a narrative of my theoretical framework and how the theme would be used to create lessons that would meet specific objectives tied to standards. These unit plans detailed the sequence of lessons, individualized and small group approaches, and the culminating activity. I also described how the culminating activity would be used to assess student learning in relation to the objectives. Although unit plans were not a requirement from my administrators, I wanted to make it clear that I understood my contractual obligation to the curriculum and to student success. However, I was going to do it in a non-traditional way. I believed that I could equalize the educational opportunities for my students through experiences and engaging learning opportunities. I was not to be deterred; I knew that academic failure was not the fault of the students and their families. It was a systemic fault. I refused to be part of that system.

A living dialogue can be achieved within the traditional one year of a grade level. However, many of the Explorers attributed the three-year loop to the power being an Explorer. Students who loop score higher on standardized tests (Burke, 1997; Cistone & Shneyderman, 2004; Sterling, 2011). Higher attendance, positive attitude towards school, and better teacher-student relationships are also outcomes of looping (Tourigny & Plante, 2020). Yet, principals and teachers resist it. In my experience, I had three principals refuse to allow looping. They argued that it would it disrupt teachers assignments for grade levels for those teachers who chose not to loop. One argued it would upset the grade level hallways and require teachers to move classrooms each year. So, rather than make instructional decisions based on research, decisions are made for teacher satisfaction and organizational efficiency.

Although this research project took place with urban students, it does not mean that they are the only ones who need such an education. All classrooms should allow students to participate in a living dialogue. We must stop treating children as though they are products that come off an assembly line. Giving voice, choice, and agency to students is not an ideology; it is a right (United Nations, 1989). Students have a right to be equally included in classroom instruction. Students have a right to instruction that interrogates the world they are going to inherit. Classrooms should be offering an education that Alena described as, "A great life experience mixed with learning."

References

Alexander, R.J. (2020). *A dialogic teaching companion*. New York, NY: Routledge.

Apple, M.W. (2000). Between neoliberalism and neoconservatism: Education and conservatism in a global context. In N.B. Torres (Ed.), *Globalization and education: Critical perspectives*, New York, NY: Routledge.

Asterhan, C.S.C., Howe, C., Lefstein, A., Matusov, E. & Reznitskaya, A. (2020). Controversies and consensus in dialogic teaching and learning. *Dialogic Pedagogy, An InternationalOnline Journal*, 8, S1–S15. https://dpj.pitt.edu DOI: 10.5195/dpj.2020.312.

Bakhtin, M. M. (1981). *The dialogic imagination : Four essays*. Austin, TX: University of Texas Press.

Brancaleone, D. & O'Brien, S. (2011). Educational commodification and the (economic) sign value of learning outcomes. *British Journal of Sociology of Education*, 32 (4), 501–519.

Burke, D. L. (1997). *Looping: Adding time, strengthening relationships* (Report No. EDO-PS-97-25). Champaign, IL: University of Illinois.

Cistone, P. & Shneyderman, A. (2004). Looping: An empirical evaluation. *International Journal of Education Policy, Research and Practice: Reconceptualizing Childhood Studies*, 5 (10), 47–61.

hooks, b. (1989). *Talking back: Thinking feminist, thinking Black*. Boston, MA: South End Press.

Kim, M. & Wilkinson, I.A.G. (2019). What is dialogic teaching? Constructing, deconstructing, and reconstructing a pedagogy of classroom talk. *Learning, Culture and Social Interaction*, 21, 71–86.

Knapp, M.S. (1995). Teaching for meaning in high-poverty classrooms. New York, NY: Teachers College Press.

Martens, M.L. (1999). Productive questions: Tools for supporting constructivist learning. *Science and Children*, 24–28.

Popkewtiz, T.S. (1999). Critical traditions, modernisms, and the "posts". In T.S. Popkewtiz & L. Fendler (Eds.), *Critical theories in education: Changing terrains of knowledge and politics*. New York, NY: Routledge.

Sterling, S. (2011). Transformative learning and sustainability: Sketching the conceptual ground. *Learning and Teaching in Higher Education*, 5, 17–33.

Sutter, B. & Grensjö, B. (1988). Explorative learning in the school? Experiences of local historical research by pupils. *Quarterly Newsletter of Laboratory of Human Cognition*, 10 (2), 39–54.

Tourigny, R. & Plante, I. (2020). Do students in a looping classroom get higher grades and report a better teacher-relationship than those in a traditional setting? *Educational Studies*, 46 (6), 744–759.

United Nations. (1989). Convention on the rights of children. *Document A/RES/44/25*. New York, NY: U.N General Assembly. Retrieved from http://wunrn.org/reference/pdf/Convention_Rights_Child.PDF.

Wegerif, R. (2013). *Dialogic: Education for the internet age*. New York, NY: Routledge.

Wegerif, R. (2019). *Chiasm: A dialogic research methodology*. www.rupertwegerif.name/blog/chiasm-a-dialogic-research-methdology.

Willbergh, I. (2017). The representation of reality in teaching: A "mimetic didactic" perspective on examples in plenary talk. *Scandinavian Journal of Educational Research*, 61 (5) 616–627.

Willbergh, I. & Aasebø, T.S. (2018). "Sociability before individuality": Lesson structure in lower secondary classrooms. *Journal of Curriculum Studies*, 51 (3) 293–305.

Index

agency 10, 13–16, 33–34, 114, 117
Alexander, R. 7, 108–111
architecture theory 15, 23–24, 98, 115
authority 23, 30, 34–41, 87, 91, 97–98, 101–104

belonging 49–52, 82, 90–94

choice 7, 10, 11–16
classroom activities 7–8, 45, 49, 64–67, 70–73, 84, 87, 91, 98, 110
classroom scripts: recitation script 2–4, 6, 15, 38, 107, 110; responsive/collaborative script 6–8, 10, 12–15, 104; responsive script 2, 4–6, 107
community of learners 8, 12, 26–29, 31–32, 54
control 2–3, 6, 14, 22, 30, 32, 35–38, 101–102, 112, 115–116
conversational floor 32, 35–37, 98, 101–102, 112
critical literacy 9, 39–41, 113–117

dialogic interactions 8, 11–12, 32, 37–39, 55, 85–86, 90, 94, 102, 107, 109–110, 113–114
discursive pedagogy 23–24, 33–34, 40, 50, 97–98, 114
discursive practices 32–33, 97, 99, 102

equality 11–12, 96–97

field experiences 20, 27, 74–75, 96
Foucault, M. 3, 14, 24, 30, 33–34
Freire, P. 3, 10, 14, 39

grounded theory 16, 46–48, 53; analytic memos 16, 50, 53–54; axial codes 16, 46, 49–52; open codes 16, 46, 48–49, 54; theoretical codes 16, 46, 50, 82
group identity 15, 97, 102–104, 114–115
Gutiérrez, K. 2–3, 5–8

inclusivity 10, 16, 51, 86, 94, 96–98, 110, 114
individualizing 49, 71, 73, 87–88
inquiry 20–25, 31–34, 71, 97, 113–114
interactional accomplishment 14–16, 35, 38, 40, 101–102, 104, 111–114
interactional space 8, 97

Lave, J. 3, 24, 33, 54, 100
living dialogue 16, 106–118
Lunch is Gross 9, 11–12, 35, 47, 71–72, 78, 88–89, 95–97, 102, 113

negotiating authority 39, 97, 101

participation frameworks 2–3, 15, 32, 97, 99–100, 104, 109–110, 112, 114–115
postmodern theory 15, 24, 30, 33
power 3–4, 7, 9–11, 14–15, 24, 29–34, 38–39, 52, 55, 97–98, 100, 102

regime of truth 30, 32–33, 113
relationships 3, 8, 10, 14, 16, 27, 29, 34, 38–39, 46, 49, 52, 54–55, 82–84, 86–87, 93–94, 107, 109, 113–114, 117

retrospective case study research 15, 42–44, 116
Rogoff, B. 2, 27, 29

shared repertoire of practices 27, 29
simultaneous overlapping conversation 2, 21, 112
social justice 16, 33, 52, 79, 82, 86, 90–91, 94
social learning theory 23
subjectivity 53, 55, 107

talking together 76, 94, 114
thematic units 1, 27, 29, 31, 110–116
theoretical framework 22, 50, 97–98, 116

voice 7–16, 33–34, 38–39, 42, 52–55, 64, 73, 76–80, 83, 85, 94–95, 97–99, 103, 112–114, 116–117

Wenger, E. 3, 24, 33, 54, 100

Zumthor, P. 23–24, 26, 33

For Product Safety Concerns and Information please contact our EU representative GPSR@taylorandfrancis.com
Taylor & Francis Verlag GmbH, Kaufingerstraße 24, 80331 München, Germany

www.ingramcontent.com/pod-product-compliance
Lightning Source LLC
Chambersburg PA
CBHW070555170426
43201CB00012B/1845